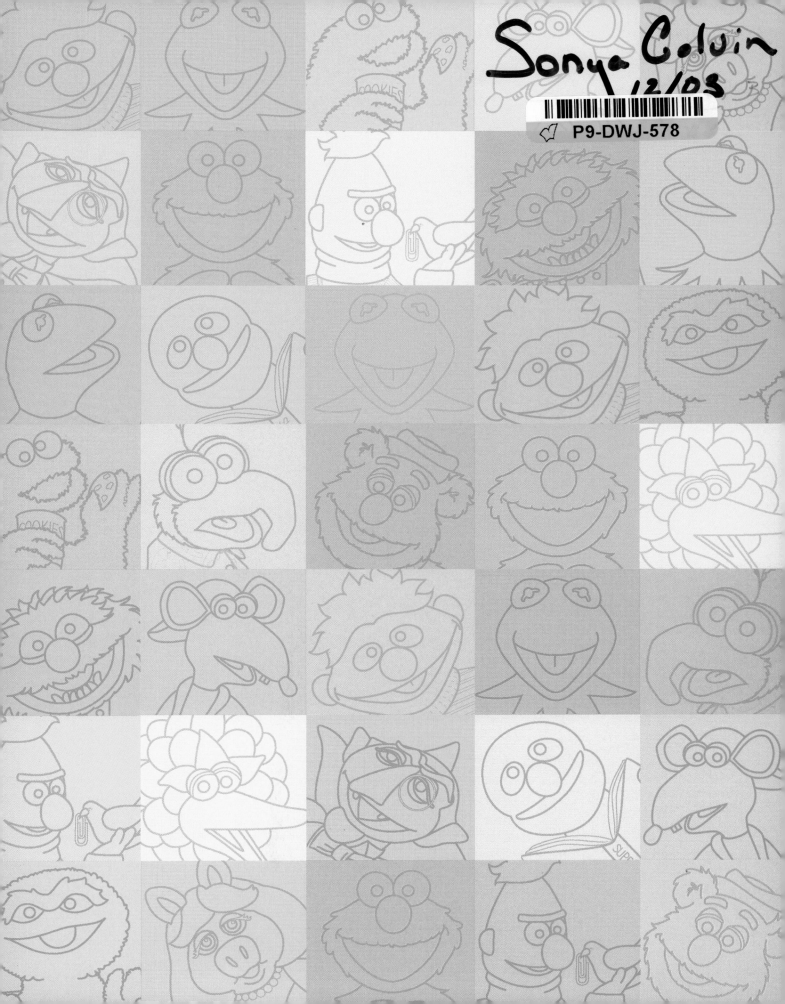

Developmental Editors: Barbara Konzak Kuhn and Lauren Attinello
The Jim Henson Company Editor: Kylie Foxx
Technical Editor: Joan Cravens
Cover Designer: Christina Jarumay
Design Director/Book Designer: Christina Jarumay
Illustrator: Aliza Kahn © C&T Publishing
Production Coordinator: Diane Pedersen
Production Assistants: Claudia Boehm, Stacy Chamness
Photography: All photography by John E. Barrett, except on pages 94, 95, 97, 98 and 108, by Richard Termine, and page 111, by Phil Jackson.

Library of Congress Cataloging-in-Publication Data
Quilting with the Muppets / The Jim Henson Company in association with Sesame Workshop.
    p. cm.
    ISBN 1-57120-101-7 (pbk.)
    1. Appliqué--Patterns. 2. Quilting--Patterns. 3. Muppet Show (Television program)
4. Sesame Street (Television program) I. The Jim Henson Company. II. Sesame Workshop.
 TT779 .Q55 2000
 746.46'041--dc21

                      00-010259
                      CIP

Published by C&T Publishing, Inc.
P.O. Box 1456
Lafayette, California 94549

Quilting with the
Muppets

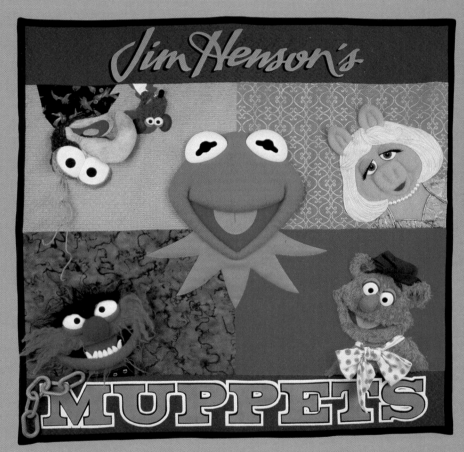

15 FUN AND CREATIVE PATTERNS

THE JIM HENSON COMPANY
IN ASSOCIATION WITH SESAME WORKSHOP

C&T PUBLISHING

Table of

Contents

Dedication

In loving memory of
Richard Hunt, Christine Moyes,
Kevin Oldham, Tom Praeger,
David Velasquez, and Jim Henson.

Acknowledgements

Many thanks to the editors, designers, and illustrators who shaped this book from an idea into a reality. And deep gratitude to John E. Barrett, Barbara S. Davis, Danielle Obinger, Connie Peterson, Stephen Rotondaro, and Polly P. Smith, for their immeasurable contributions.

Introduction

BY CHERYL HENSON

The quilts in this book were made by the artists and craftspeople who design, build, and costume the Muppet puppets in The Muppet Workshop, and by some of their friends in the extended Muppet family, such as art directors and puppeteers. Most of the quilts were made for specific people to mark a special event. Each quilt square is a gift of sharing. The eclectic mix of material and techniques used by the different quilters combine beautifully to make these friendship quilts unique.

A few years ago, we made a quilt to celebrate Sesame Street's 30th Anniversary to be auctioned for charity. It was the only time that a quilt was to leave the immediate family of Muppet friends. I chose Kermit the Frog for my square because my father, Jim Henson, had created and performed Kermit. Kermit was almost an alter ego for my father. He was the calm, self-reflective one in the middle of the otherwise crazy, chaotic world of the Muppets. In the square, Kermit gestures to a number five which I chose because there are five children in our family. My father enjoyed including his family in his work, and so the people he worked with often felt like family. He also created the first animated number films for "Sesame Street" and my favorite was the one that sang, "Five, Five, Five, Five, Let's sing a song of Five. How many is Five?"

Within my father's own family there is a long history of quilting and needlework. We cherish the wonderful quilts and handwork that were made by my great-aunts, grandmother, and great-grandmother. My father always appreciated the extraordinary skill and care that went into them and I am sure that he would be delighted by all of the quilts in this book, particularly as they were made as gifts of friendship.

— CHERYL HENSON

30 Years of Our Sesame Street Family quilt

General Instructions

■ USING THE BLOCK PATTERNS

The instructions given for each of the Muppet blocks are for fusible, flat appliqué. Using fusible appliqué and washable cotton fabric to create the blocks allows for the quilt to be used as a baby quilt. You may add embellishments to each block as desired, with regard to safety considerations and the intended use and recipient of the quilt. (Tips are given within each of the instructions for adding embellishments or for alternative construction methods.) If you have the experience and desire to add dimension to the characters (sculpting foam for a face, for example), you will need to use additional fabric to cover any filler you add. Follow the manufacturer's guidelines for any materials and alternative construction methods if adding dimension or embellishments to the blocks. Note that these blocks might not be machine-washable, based on the varied use of multiple construction methods and materials.

For each of the blocks, a pattern of the Muppet is drawn within a 7 1/2" square (which will be the finished size, when sewn, of the block). The Muppet is drawn within the square to best duplicate the placement in the original block, but you may increase the size of each character within the block to better match the group of blocks in your quilt.

■ TRANSFERRING THE PATTERN PIECES

The appliqué shapes are printed actual size within the block pattern for each Muppet. You will first need to separate and then reverse the shapes from the patterns. If you are familiar with tracing patterns from a book, and have a favorite method, we encourage you to use the method you are most comfortable with. If you are new to quilting, use the following methods as a guide.

Each of the project instructions lists steps for preparing the fusible adhesive. You will need to trace the pattern pieces from the book to obtain each shape. Begin by placing a piece of tracing paper over the block pattern. Using a #2 pencil, carefully trace the pattern shape onto the paper. (If you prefer, you can trace each shape individually onto separate pieces of tracing paper.) Be sure to trace any dashed lines for top-stitching placement. You will then need to trace the shapes and top-stitching lines from the tracing paper onto the fusible appliqué.

Although the steps in the block instructions call for tracing paper, you may also make a photocopy of the pattern, turn it face down onto a lightbox, and trace the shapes from the back of the photocopy directly onto the fusible adhesive.

■ THE BACKGROUND BLOCK

Cut the background block 8" square to add an extra 1/4" on all sides for the seam allowance. For pieces of the patterns that overlap the edge of the block, such as Fozzie Bear's bowtie (page 20), you will need to sew the blocks together before fusing the overlapping pattern pieces in place.

When choosing the color of fabric for the background square, use the background fabric shown in the original square as a guide. You may change the fabric colors as desired, but try to keep to colors which best suit the Muppet character. Again, the choice of washable 100% cotton fabric is best. Cotton fabric shifts less than other fabrics, and is of heavier weight and durability. You may also piece together assorted fabrics to create an interesting background combination.

■ USING FAKE FUR

"Fake fur" is the generic name used for various types of pile, which is soft, dimensional fabric. Common types of fake fur have cotton backing with spun rayon facing. The warp (lengthwise) yarns carry the extra threads which create the "fur" pile face. The fabric often has a one-way direction, and care must be taken when cutting the fabric to work in the direction of the pile.

You may wish to use fake fur to mimic the original Muppet character, or to add accents such as hair and eyebrows. If you choose to use fake fur, follow these basic guidelines:

For those blocks where adding fake fur is appropriate, you will need to examine specific areas of the pieces that overlap each other. Using the Cookie Monster block (page 44) as an example, the mouth, eyes, jar, and cookie will look best when they are inserted underneath the fur fabric, where shapes have been cut for them to appear.

To start, first cut each pattern piece from the back or "wrong side" of the fabric, where the flat surface supports drawing the outline shape of the pattern. You will then need to mark the areas where the mouth, eyes, jar, and cookie will overlap with head, body, and hands. Mark these additional outlines on the back of the fabric, matching the shapes carefully to avoid gaps in the final placement of all the pattern pieces.

Cut the pieces carefully from the back of the fabric, avoiding clipping the fur. The fur will separate nicely once the back is cut.

For machine appliqué, turn the cut fur-pieces right side up. Carefully clip away a narrow (1/16" wide) strip of fur along the edge (leaving the backing intact) so you may easily machine satin-stitch the piece in place. Insert the mouth, eyes, jar, and cookie pieces under the fake fur fabric and tack in place, as desired.

Begin satin stitching around the edges where the pieces overlap. Satin stitch the raw edges using the same color thread as the fur pile (see Satin Stitching, right).

To hand-appliqué fake fur pieces, add a ¼" seam allowance around each piece to tuck under as you stitch (to keep the pieces from unraveling). Add ¼" seam allowances to all overlapping areas of the character. For these areas, first slip-stitch the fake fur to the underlying appliqué piece before fusing the assembled piece to the background block fabric.

◼ APPLIQUÉ ORDER

Once the necessary overlapping pieces are in place, fuse them to the background block, using the Appliqué Order as a guide. Please note that the Appliqué Order reflects the use of flat, appliqué pieces, rather than fake fur, numbered in order of placement on the block background. You will need to review the Appliqué Order based on your use of fake fur for some of the pattern pieces. In general, any underlying shape, such as the mouth and eyes, should be added under the fake fur piece before fusing the assembled piece to the background. The hair and eyebrows of a character should be fused last, using the same color thread as the fur to satin stitch the edges.

◼ SATIN STITCHING

Satin stitches are rows of close, parallel stitches which are commonly used to cover the edges of a pattern piece, or may be used to fill a small shape, such as the eye pupils. The completed stitches should have a smooth "satin" look to enhance the design. Most modern sewing machines have built-in settings for satin stitching. Follow the manufacturer's instructions for your brand of sewing machine. You may also use embroidery thread and a needle to add details or highlights, as desired. However, if you are stitching by hand, it is important to add the detail stitching prior to final assembly of the block, since the fusible appliqué may be too stiff or difficult to pierce with the needle.

◼ TIPS

Tips are given for each block. Many of the tips refer to the construction of the original block, to help you understand how the designer created it. The tips are meant to provide you with insightful suggestions for embellishing or refining your blocks. You may need to consult your local crafts-shop specialist or quilt instructor, or refer to manufacturer's product instructions, for alternative construction techniques and materials.

How to Organize a Friendship Quilt

1. Choose an event.

2. Ask friends to be involved; determine the number of participants.

3. Determine block size, quilt colors, and block due date.

4. Choose fabrics.

5. Notify all participants of block size, quilt colors, due date; send fabrics to those who need them; remind everyone to leave plenty of seam allowance.

6. Send a reminder two weeks prior to the due date.

7. Assemble blocks into quilt.

8. Collect money if it is to be quilted by a professional, or quilt yourself.

Kermit the Frog

Materials Needed:

Fabric & Notions
8" square colorful fabric for background
6" square light green fabric for collar
4" square red fabric for mouth interior
3" square pink fabric for tongue
6" square green fabric for face
4" square white fabric for eyes
3" square black fabric for pupils

Tools & Supplies
Tracing paper, #2 pencil, scissors, 8" square tear-away stabilizer, fusible adhesive with paper backing for each shape, iron

Preparing Fusible Appliqué

The appliqué shapes are printed actual size within the block pattern, page 14. You will need to separate the shapes within the block before tracing them onto the paper-side of the fusible adhesive (noting where the shapes overlap). Refer to the General Instructions, pages 10-11, for tips on using the block patterns.

1 Lay a sheet of tracing paper over the block pattern. Using a #2 pencil, carefully trace each shape onto the paper. If you prefer, trace each shape onto separate pieces of paper. Be sure to trace any dashed top-stitching lines.

2 Cut the shapes from the tracing paper and flip them over (reversing the shape) onto the paper-side of the adhesive. Trace the reversed shapes onto the adhesive, again marking any top-stitching placement lines.

3 Cut the shapes from the adhesive, leaving an edge of approximately 1/4" around the solid traced lines.

4 Following the manufacturer's instructions for fusing, iron the cut shapes paper-side up onto the wrong side of the fabric. The color of each shape is shown in the Appliqué Order.

5 Cut the shapes from the newly fused fabric along the marked solid lines on each appliqué. Transfer any top-stitching lines to the right side of the fabric.

T I P S

☐ *The original Kermit block has a sculpted base of foam, covered with green fleece. The instructions given for the block are for fusible, flat appliqué. If you choose to use additional materials to add dimension, you will need to increase the fabric amounts accordingly.*

☐ *For your Kermit quilt block, the best choice of fabric is 100% cotton fabric. If you choose to use fleece, note that the fabric tends to shift easily.*

☐ *Choosing the right color of green fabric for Kermit is key to making your quilt block look authentic. If the color choice is between a darker fabric and a lighter one, choose the lighter fabric. The lighter tone will enliven a colorful quilt.*

Kermit block is a 7 ½" square when sewn.

QUILTING WITH THE **MUPPETS**

Fusing the Appliqué Shapes

1 Using the block photograph and pattern (page 14) as a guide for correct placement, remove the paper backing and position the appliqué shapes fabric-side up (in the numbered order) onto the block background square. Dashed lines indicate top-stitching lines. Note that the background square includes the 1/4" seam allowance.

2 When you are satisfied with the placement, iron the pieces into place following the manufacturer's instructions.

Satin-Stitch Appliqué (Optional)

1 Refer to General Instructions, pages 10-11, for tips on satin stitching. Place an 8" piece of tear-away stabilizer under the block, matching all edges.

2 Using a fairly narrow stitch and thread meant for machine appliqué, stitch around the appliqué shapes. Keep your stitch length as short as possible. Stitch over the raw edges of the fused appliqué shapes to cover them. When completed, the stitching should have a smooth "satin" look.

Appliqué Order

1 Light Green: collar

2 Red: mouth interior

3 Pink: tongue

4 Green: face

5 White: eyes

6 Black: pupils

Miss Piggy

Materials Needed:

Fabric & Notions

8" square colorful fabric for background block
8" square peach fabric for chest, face, nose, and ears
1" square red fabric for mouth interior
3" square white fabric for eyes
2" square blue fabric for irises
2" square lavender fabric for eyelids
3" square black fabric for pupils and eyelashes
4" square aqua fabric for dress
7" satin piping for dress, see Tips (optional)
9" square yellow fabric for hair
4" square white fabric or fake pearls for necklace, see Tips

Tools & Supplies

Tracing paper, #2 pencil, scissors, 8" square tear-away stabilizer, fusible adhesive with paper backing for each shape, iron

Preparing Fusible Appliqué

The appliqué shapes are printed actual size within the block pattern, page 18. You will need to separate the shapes within the block before tracing them onto the paper-side of the fusible adhesive (noting where the shapes overlap). Refer to the General Instructions, pages 10-11, for tips on using the block patterns.

1 Lay a sheet of tracing paper over the block pattern. Using a #2 pencil, carefully trace each shape onto the paper. If you prefer, trace each shape onto separate pieces of paper. Be sure to trace any dashed top-stitching lines.

2 Cut the shapes from the tracing paper and flip them over (reversing the shape) onto the paper-side of the adhesive. Trace the reversed shapes onto the adhesive, again marking any top-stitching placement lines.

3 Cut the shapes from the adhesive, leaving an edge of approximately 1/4" around the solid traced lines.

4 Following the manufacturer's instructions for fusing, iron the cut shapes paper-side up onto the wrong side of the fabric. The color of each shape is shown in the Appliqué Order.

5 Cut the shapes from the newly fused fabric along the marked solid lines of each appliqué. Transfer any top-stitching lines to the right side of the fabric.

T I P S

■ The original Miss Piggy block was padded to add dimension. Miss Piggy's nose, cheeks, lip, and ears were carved from foam, then covered with fleece. The directions for the block, however, are for a flat, appliqué block. If you wish to add dimension to your block, you will need to increase the fabric amounts accordingly.

■ Miss Piggy's hair was made of satin, batting, and muslin, all stitched together using a trapunto technique. Two different colors of rattail cord are stitched into her hair as highlights. Miss Piggy's bangs were made separately and applied on top of her hair.

■ The necklace was made of buttons, each stitched into place. You may also tack on a strand of fake pearls or, if making a baby quilt, appliqué dots of white fabric.

■ You may use embroidery or satin stitching to create Miss Piggy's pupils. Use a dark color for the pupil, then add a white or light color for highlights.

Miss Piggy block is a 7 ¹/₂" square when sewn.

Fusing the Appliqué Shapes

1 Using the block photograph and pattern (page 18) as a guide for correct placement, remove the paper backing and position the appliqué shapes fabric side up (in the numbered order) onto the block background square. Dashed lines indicate top-stitching lines. Note that the background square includes the 1/4" seam allowance.

2 When you are satisfied with the placement, iron the pieces into place following the manufacturer's instructions.

Satin-Stitch Appliqué (Optional)

1 Place an 8" piece of tear-away stabilizer under the block, matching all edges.

2 With your sewing machine set for a closely-spaced satin stitch, and using thread meant for machine appliqué, stitch around the appliqué shapes. Because Miss Piggy's block has narrow or small appliqués such as the eyes, eyelashes, and eyelids, use a narrow stitch to avoid overwhelming the appliqué. Stitch over the raw edges of the fused appliqué shapes to cover them. When completed, the stitching should have a smooth "satin" look.

Appliqué Order

1 **2** **4** **13** Peach: chest, face, nose, ears

3 Red: mouth interior

5 White: eyes

6 Blue: irises

7 Lavender: eyelids

8 **9** Black: pupils, eyelashes

10 **11** **12** Print: dress

14 **15** **16** Yellow: hair

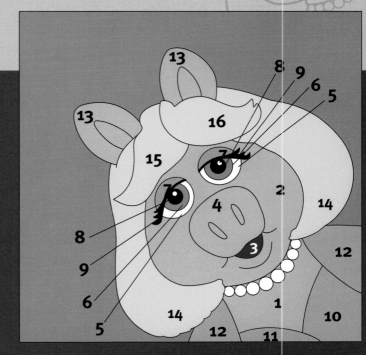

Fozzie Bear

Materials Needed:

Fabric & Notions

8" square colorful fabric for block background

9" square golden brown fabric, fleece, or fake fur for face, ears, and body

4" square red fabric for mouth interior

4" square dark pink fabric for nose

3" square pink fabric for tongue

3" square lavender fabric for eyelids

9" square dark brown fabric for eyelines and hat

4" square white fabric for eyes

3" square black fabric for pupils

4" square dark brown fabric, fleece, or fake fur for eyebrows

Premade bowtie with tails, see Tips

Felt hat, see Tips

Tools & Supplies

Tracing paper, #2 pencil, scissors, 8" square tear-away stabilizer, fusible adhesive with paper backing for each shape, iron

Preparing Fusible Appliqué

The appliqué shapes are printed actual size within the block pattern, page 22. You will need to separate the shapes within the block before tracing them onto the paper-side of the fusible adhesive (noting where the shapes overlap). Refer to the General Instructions, pages 10-11, for tips on using the block patterns.

1 Lay a sheet of tracing paper over the block pattern. Using a #2 pencil, carefully trace each shape onto the paper. If you prefer, trace each shape onto separate pieces of paper. Be sure to trace any dashed top-stitching lines.

2 Cut the shapes from the tracing paper and flip them over (reversing the shape) onto the paper-side of the adhesive. Trace the reversed shapes onto the adhesive, again marking any top-stitching placement lines.

3 Cut the shapes from the adhesive, leaving an edge of approximately 1/4" around the solid traced lines.

4 Following the manufacturer's instructions for fusing, iron the cut shapes paper-side up onto the wrong side of the fabric. The color of each shape is shown in the Appliqué Order.

5 Cut the shapes from the newly fused fabric along the marked solid lines of each appliqué. Transfer any top-stitching lines to the right side of the fabric.

TIPS

The original Fozzie block was made with fabrics that were used to make the Muppet. The instructions given for this block are for fusible, flat appliqué. If you choose to use additional materials to add dimension, you will need to increase the fabric amounts accordingly.

■ If using a premade hat for Fozzie, you may need to trim the hat to lay flat, then tack it on accordingly. Small felt hats for dolls or hats for children and adults, cut to size, are ideal.

■ Fozzie's bowtie should be a premade tie; tack the ends on carefully to add dimension. If the quilt is for a small child, adding a bow that can be tied and untied can help strengthen motor skills for developing hands.

■ If you choose to use fake fur to best duplicate Fozzie Bear's characteristic fuzziness, follow the guidelines on pages 10-11.

Fozzie block is a 7 ½" square when sewn.

Fusing the Appliqué Shapes

1 Using the block photograph and pattern (page 22) as a guide for correct placement, remove the paper backing and position the appliqué shapes fabric side up (in the numbered order) onto the block background square. Dashed lines indicate top-stitching lines. Note that the background square includes the ¹/₄" seam allowance.

2 When you are satisfied with the placement, iron the pieces into place following the manufacturer's instructions. If you are adding a felt hat to the block, you will need to cut some of the parts of the hat to fit around the ears and on top of the head, then iron it into place.

Satin-Stitch Appliqué (Optional)

1 Refer to General Instructions, pages 10-11, for tips on satin stitching. Place an 8" piece of tear-away stabilizer under the block, matching all edges.

2 Using a fairly narrow stitch and thread meant for machine appliqué, stitch around the appliqué shapes. Keep your stitch length as close as possible. Stitch over the raw edges of the fused appliqué shapes to cover them. When completed, the stitching should have a smooth "satin" look.

Appliqué Order

1 **2** **5** Golden Brown: face, ears, and body

3 Red: mouth interior

4 Dark Pink: nose

6 Pink: tongue

7 Lavender: eyelids

8 **11** Dark Brown: eyelines, eyebrows

9 White: eyes

10 Black: pupils

12 Print: bowtie

13 Dark Brown: hat

Animal

QUILTING WITH THE **MUPPETS**

Materials Needed:

Fabric & Notions
8" square colorful fabric for block background
5" square black fabric for mouth interior and pupils
5" square red fabric for tongue and nose
5" square white fabric for teeth and eyes
9" square magenta fabric, fleece, or fake fur for head
5" square black fabric, fleece, or fake fur for eyebrows
8" square orange fabric for lower eyelids and bottom lip
Premade dog or cat collar, or black ribbon, see Tips
Silver embroidery thread, see Tips (optional: plastic chain)

Tools & Supplies
Tracing paper, #2 pencil, scissors, 8" square tear-away stabilizer, fusible adhesive with paper backing for each shape, iron

Preparing Fusible Appliqué

The appliqué shapes are printed actual size within the block pattern, page 26. You will need to separate the shapes within the block before tracing them onto the paper-side of the fusible adhesive (noting where the shapes overlap). Refer to the General Instructions, pages 10-11, for tips on using the block patterns.

1 Lay a sheet of tracing paper over the block pattern. Using a #2 pencil, carefully trace each shape onto the paper. If you prefer, trace each shape onto separate pieces of paper. Be sure to trace any dashed top-stitching lines.

2 Cut the shapes from the tracing paper and flip them over (reversing the shape) onto the paper-side of the adhesive. Trace the reversed shapes onto the adhesive, again marking any top-stitching placement lines.

3 Cut the shapes from the adhesive, leaving an edge of approximately 1/4" around the solid traced lines.

4 Following the manufacturer's instructions for fusing, iron the cut shapes paper-side up onto the wrong side of the fabric. The color of each shape is shown in the Appliqué Order.

5 Cut the shapes from the newly fused fabric along the marked solid lines of each appliqué. Transfer any top-stitching lines to the right side of the fabric.

T I P S

The instructions given for the block are for fusible, flat appliqué. If you choose to use additional materials to add dimension, you will need to increase the fabric amounts accordingly.

■ You may use a small dog or cat collar for Animal's collar, but you will need to trim it to lay flat. You may also substitute a black ribbon, and embroider the studs with silver thread. If you choose to add a plastic chain, be sure to tack it into place.

■ If you choose to use fake fur to best duplicate Animal's characteristic shagginess, follow the guidelines for fake fur on pages 10-11.

Animal block is a 7 ¹/₂" square when sewn.

QUILTING WITH THE **MUPPETS**

Fusing the Appliqué Shapes

1 Using the block photograph and pattern (page 26) as a guide for correct placement, remove the paper backing and position all appliqué shapes fabric-side up (in the numbered order) onto the block background square. Note that the background square includes the 1/4" seam allowance.

2 When you are satisfied with the placement, iron the pieces into place following the manufacturer's instructions. If you are adding a dog or cat collar, or black ribbon, you will need to position part of it under the head accordingly.

Optional: Satin-Stitch Appliqué

1 Refer to the General Instructions, pages 10-11, for tips on satin stitching. Place an 8" piece of tear-away stabilizer under block, matching all edges.

2 Using a fairly narrow stitch and thread meant for machine appliqué, stitch around the appliqué shapes. Keep your stitch length as close as possible. Stitch over the raw edges of the fused appliqué shapes to cover them. When completed, the stitching should have a smooth "satin" look.

Appliqué Order

1 **8** **11** Black: mouth interior, pupils, collar

2 **9** Red: tongue, nose

3 White: teeth

4 Magenta: head

5 Black: eyebrows

6 White: eyes

7 **10** Orange: lower eyelids, bottom lip

Gonzo

QUILTING WITH THE **MUPPETS**

Materials Needed:

Fabric & Notions
8" square colorful fabric for block background
8" square colorful print fabric for shirt
4" square dark blue fabric for head
6" square light blue fabric for lip and nose
4" square red fabric for mouth interior
3" square pink fabric for tongue
4" square yellow fabric for upper eyelids
6" square white fabric for eyes
5" square green fabric for eyelines
3" square black fabric for pupils
36" thin purple tubing for hair
2 buttons for shirt print

Tools & Supplies
Tracing paper, #2 pencil, scissors, 8" square tear-away stabilizer, fusible adhesive with paper backing for each shape, iron

Preparing Fusible Appliqué

The appliqué shapes are printed actual size within the block pattern, page 30. You will need to separate the shapes within the block before tracing them onto the paper-side of the fusible adhesive (noting where the shapes overlap). Refer to the General Instructions, pages 10-11, for tips on using the block patterns.

1 Lay a sheet of tracing paper over the block pattern. Using a #2 pencil, carefully trace each shape onto the paper. If you prefer, trace each shape onto separate pieces of paper. Be sure to trace any dashed top-stitching lines.

2 Cut the shapes from the tracing paper and flip them over (reversing the shape) onto the paper-side of the adhesive. Trace the reversed shapes onto the adhesive, again marking any top-stitching placement lines.

3 Cut the shapes from the adhesive, leaving an edge of approximately 1/4" around the solid traced lines.

4 Following the manufacturer's instructions for fusing, iron the cut shapes paper-side up onto the wrong side of the fabric. The color of each shape is shown in the Appliqué Order.

5 Cut the shapes from the newly fused fabric along the marked solid lines of each appliqué. Transfer any top-stitching lines to the right side of the fabric.

The original Gonzo block was made with fabrics used for the Muppet. The eyes are plastic disks covered with stretch velour fabric. The nose is carved foam, which was lightly glued on, then stitched in place. The instructions given for the block are for fusible, flat appliqué. If you choose to use additional materials to add dimension, you will need to increase the fabric amounts accordingly.

Purple acrylic paint was sponged on sparingly to add high-lights and shadows to Gonzo's face. If you wish, you can use acrylic paints/dyes to create a similar effect.

Gonzo block is a 7 $\frac{1}{2}$" square when sewn.

Fusing the Appliqué Shapes

1 Using the block photograph and pattern (page 30) as a guide for correct placement, remove the paper backing and position the appliqué shapes fabric-side up (in the numbered order) onto the block background square. Dashed lines indicate top-stitching lines. Note that the background square includes the $1/4$" seam allowance.

2 When you are satisfied with the placement, iron the pieces into place following manufacturer's instructions. If you choose to add hair to the block, trim the thin purple tubing into several pieces of different length, then lay the pieces underneath the eyes before ironing the eyes into place. Tack the tubing down, as necessary. If you'd like to add buttons to Gonzo's shirt, simply hand sew them to the shirt where shown on the diagram.

Satin-Stitch Appliqué (Optional)

1 Refer to the General Instructions, pages 10-11, for tips on satin stitching. Place an 8" piece of tear-away stabilizer under block, matching all edges.

2 Using a fairly narrow stitch and thread meant for machine appliqué, stitch around the appliqué shapes. Keep your stitch length as short as possible. Stitch over the raw edges of the fused appliqué shapes to cover them. When completed, the stitching should have a smooth "satin" look.

Appliqué Order

1 2 3 5 Print: shirt

4 Dark Blue: head

6 9 Light Blue: lip, nose

7 Red: mouth interior

8 Pink: tongue

10 Yellow: eyelids

11 White: eyes

12 Green: eyelines

13 Black: pupis

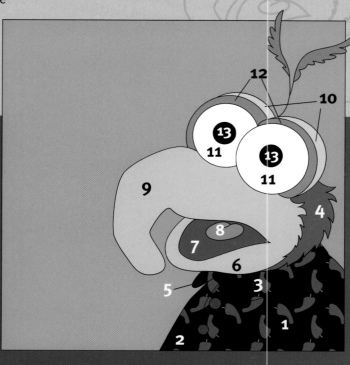

Rizzo
the Rat

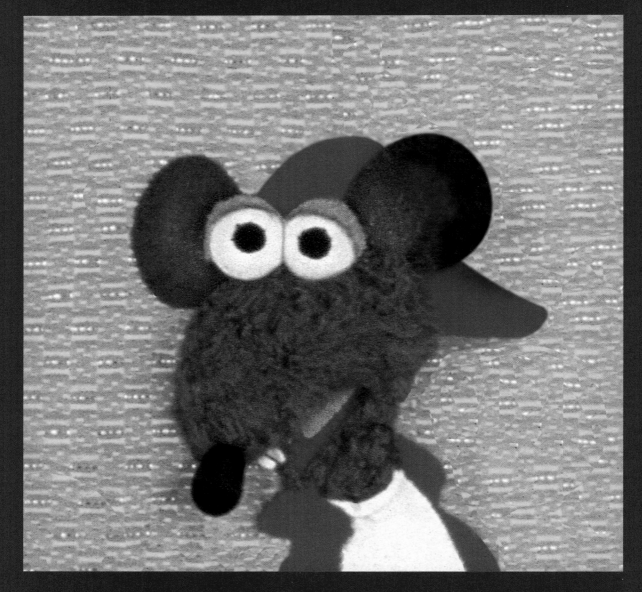

Materials Needed:

Fabric & Notions

8" square colorful fabric for block background

6" square white fabric for eyes and T-shirt

7" square red fabric for jacket, mouth interior, and hat

5" square brown fabric for neck, lower lip, ears, and face

3" square pink fabric for tongue

4" square light pink fabric for inner ears

3" square black fabric for pupils

2 small strips white felt for teeth

3" square lavender fabric for eyelids

4" square black fabric or embroidery thread for nose, see Tips

Tools & Supplies

Tracing paper, #2 pencil, scissors, 8" square tear-away stabilizer, fusible adhesive with paper backing for each shape, iron

Preparing Fusible Appliqué

The appliqué shapes are printed actual size within the block pattern, page 34. You will need to separate the shapes within the block before tracing them onto the paper-side of the fusible adhesive (noting where the shapes overlap). Refer to the General Instructions, pages 10-11, for tips on using the block patterns.

1 Lay a sheet of tracing paper over the block pattern. Using a #2 pencil, carefully trace each shape onto the paper. If you prefer, trace each shape onto separate pieces of paper. Be sure to trace any dashed top-stitching lines.

2 Cut the shapes from the tracing paper and flip them over (reversing the shape) onto the paper-side of the adhesive. Trace the reversed shapes onto the adhesive, again marking any top-stitching placement lines.

3 Cut the shapes from the adhesive, leaving an edge of approximately 1/4" around the solid traced lines.

4 Following the manufacturer's instructions for fusing, iron the cut shapes paper-side up onto the wrong side of the fabric. The color of each shape is shown in the Appliqué Order.

5 Cut the shapes from the newly fused fabric along the marked solid lines of each appliqué. Transfer any top-stitching lines to the right side of the fabric.

The instructions given for the block are for fusible, flat appliqué. If you choose to use additional materials to add dimension, you will need to increase the fabric amounts accordingly.

■ *The nose looks best when embroidered or appliquéd on. You may, however, substitute a button for the nose, so long as the quilt is not for a small child.*

■ *If you'd like to use fake fur to duplicate Rizzo's characteristic fuzziness, follow the guidelines on pages 10-11.*

Rizzo block is a 7 $\frac{1}{2}$" square when sewn.

QUILTING WITH THE MUPPETS

Fusing the Appliqué Shapes

1 Using the block photograph and pattern (page 34) as a guide for correct placement, remove the paper backing and position the appliqué shapes fabric-side up (in the numbered order) onto the block background square. Dashed lines indicate top-stitching lines. Note that the background square includes the 1/4" seam allowance.

2 When you are satisfied with the placement, iron the pieces into place. Embroider the nose with a satin stitch or, if using a button, hand-stitch it into place with matching thread.

Satin-Stitch Appliqué (Optional)

1 Refer to the General Instructions, pages 10-11, for tips on satin stitching. Place an 8" piece of tear-away stabilizer under the block, matching all edges.

2 Using a fairly narrow stitch and thread meant for machine appliqué, stitch around the appliqué shapes. Keep your stitch length as short as possible. Stitch over the raw edges of the fused appliqué shapes to cover them. When completed, the stitching should have a smooth "satin" look.

Appliqué Order

1 **10** **13**	White: T-shirt, eyes, teeth
2 **6**	Red: jacket, hat
3 **7**	Brown: face, ears
4	Red: mouth interior
5	Pink: tongue
8	Light Pink: inner ears
9 **12**	Black: nose, pupils
11	Lavender: eyelids

Ernie

QUILTING WITH THE **MUPPETS**

Materials Needed:

Fabric & Notions

8" square colorful print for block background
8" square horizontal-stripe print for shirt
5" square yellow fabric for collar
9" square orange fabric for ears and face
6" square red fabric for mouth interior and nose
3" square pink fabric for tongue
4" square white fabric for eyes
3" square black fabric for pupils
6" square black fabric or fake fur for hair
Orange embroidery thread (optional)

Tools & Supplies

Tracing paper, #2 pencil, scissors, 8" square tear-away stabilizer, fusible adhesive with paper backing for each shape, iron

Preparing Fusible Appliqué

The appliqué shapes are printed actual size within the block pattern, page 38. You will need to separate the shapes within the block before tracing them onto the paper-side of the fusible adhesive (noting where the shapes overlap). Refer to the General Instructions, pages 10-11, for tips on using the block patterns.

1 Lay a sheet of tracing paper over the block pattern. Using a #2 pencil, carefully trace each shape onto the paper. If you prefer, trace each shape onto separate pieces of paper. Be sure to trace any dashed top-stitching lines.

2 Cut the shapes from the tracing paper and flip them over (reversing the shape) onto the paper-side of the adhesive. Trace the reversed shapes onto the adhesive, again marking any top-stitching placement lines.

3 Cut the shapes from the adhesive, leaving an edge of approximately ¹/₄" around the solid traced lines.

4 Following the manufacturer's instructions for fusing, iron the cut shapes paper-side up onto the wrong side of the fabric. The color of each shape is shown in the Appliqué Order.

5 Cut the shapes from the newly fused fabric along the marked solid lines of each appliqué. Transfer any top-stitching lines to the right side of the fabric.

T I P S

The instructions given for the Ernie block are for fusible, flat appliqué. If you choose to use additional materials to add dimension, you will need to increase the fabric amounts accordingly.

You may want to use fake fur to best imitate Ernie's fuzzy hair. Follow the guidelines on pages 10-11.

If satin stitching is used, satin stitch the smile lines at the corners of Ernie's mouth. This could also be embroidered by hand with orange embroidery thread.

Ernie block is a 7 ¹/₂" square when sewn.

Fusing the Appliqué Shapes

1. Using the block photograph and pattern (page 38) as a guide for correct placement, remove the paper backing and position the appliqué shapes fabric-side up (in the numbered order) onto the block background square. Dashed lines indicate top-stitching lines. Note that the background square includes the 1/4" seam allowance.

2. When you are satisfied with the placement, iron the pieces into place following the manufacturer's instructions.

Satin-Stitch Appliqué (Optional)

1. Refer to the General Instructions, pages 10-11, for tips on satin stitching. Place an 8" piece of tear-away stabilizer under the block, matching all edges.

2. Using a fairly narrow stitch and thread meant for machine appliqué, stitch around the appliqué shapes. Keep your stitch length as short as possible. Stitch over the raw edges of the fused appliqué shapes to cover them. When completed, the stitching should have a smooth "satin" look.

Appliqué Order

1		Stripe: shirt
2		Yellow: collar
3	**4**	Orange: ears, face
5	**7**	Red: mouth interior, nose
6		Pink: tongue
8		White: eyes
9	**10**	Black: pupils, hair

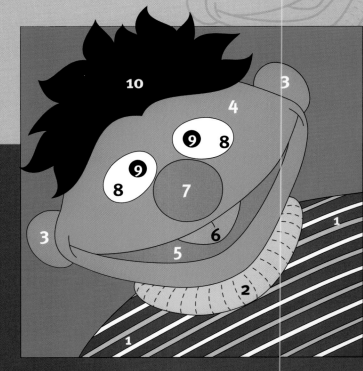

The Count

Materials Needed:

Fabric & Notions

8" square colorful fabric print for block background

15" square black fabric for coat, lapel, sleeve, hair, mouth interior, pupils, eyelines, beard, and eyebrows

5" square yellow fabric for lower sash

5" square red fabric for upper sash

10" square white fabric for shirt, collar, bowtie, sleeves, teeth, and eyes

9" square green fabric for cape

14" square purple fabric for neck, hands, ears, face, eyelids, and nose

3" square magenta fabric for tongue

Silver soutache for monocle

2 white buttons for shirt

Tools & Supplies

Tracing paper, #2 pencil, scissors, 8" square tear-away stablizer, fusible adhesive with paper backing for each shape, iron

Preparing Fusible Appliqué

The appliqué shapes are printed actual size within the block pattern, page 42. You will need to separate the shapes within the block before tracing them onto the paper-side of the fusible adhesive (noting where the shapes overlap). Refer to the General Instructions, pages 10-11, for tips on using the block patterns.

1 Lay a sheet of tracing paper over the block pattern. Using a #2 pencil, carefully trace each shape onto the paper. If you prefer, trace each shape onto separate pieces of paper. Be sure to trace any dashed top-stitching lines.

2 Cut the shapes from the tracing paper and flip them over (reversing the shape) onto the paper-side of the adhesive. Trace the reversed shapes onto the adhesive, again marking any top-stitching placement lines.

3 Cut the shapes from the adhesive, leaving an edge of approximately 1/4" around the solid traced lines.

4 Following the manufacturer's instructions for fusing, iron the cut shapes paper-side up onto the wrong side of the fabric. The color of each shape is shown in the Appliqué Order.

5 Cut the shapes from the newly fused fabric along the marked solid lines of each appliqué. Transfer any top-stitching lines to the right side of the fabric.

T I P S

The instructions given for the Count block are for fusible, flat appliqué. If you choose to use additional materials to add dimension, you will need to increase the fabric amounts accordingly.

■ *You may prefer to use a pre-made white bowtie, rather than fuse the pattern pieces to the block. Tack the bowtie in place before adding the beard.*

The Count block is a 7 ½" square when sewn.

Fusing the Appliqué Shapes

1 Using the block photograph and pattern (page 42) as a guide for correct placement, remove the paper backing and position the appliqué shapes fabric-side up (in the numbered order) onto the block background square. Dashed lines indicate top-stitching lines. Note that the background square includes the 1/4" seam allowance.

2 When you are satisfied with the placement, iron the pieces into place following the manufacturer's instructions. Stitch on the soutache in a circle to form the monocle. Tack on the buttons.

Satin-Stitch Appliqué (Optional)

1 Refer to the General Instructions, pages 10-11, for tips on satin stitching. Place an 8" piece of tear-away stabilizer under the block, matching all edges.

2 Using a narrow stitch and thread meant for machine appliqué, stitch around the appliqué shapes. Keep your stitch length as short as possible. Stitch over the raw edges of the fused appliqué shapes to cover them. When completed, the stitching should have a smooth "satin" look.

Appliqué Order

1 Black: coat

2 Yellow: lower sash

3 Red: upper sash

4 7 10 11 14 21 22
White: shirt, collar, bowtie, sleeves, teeth, eyes

5 8 16 Green: cape

6 13 15 17 23 24 27
Purple: neck, hands, ears, face, eyelids, nose

9 12 18 19 25 26 28 29
Black: lapels, sleeves, hair, mouth interior, pupils, eyelines, beard, eyebrows

20 Magenta: tongue

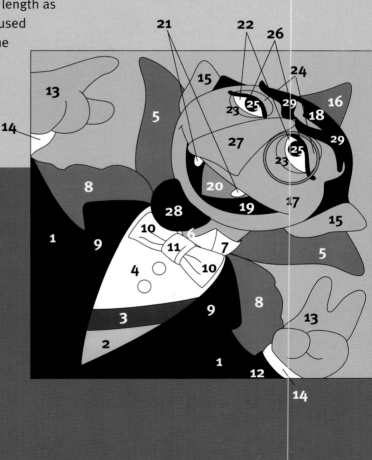

Cookie Monster

Materials Needed:

Fabric & Notions

8" square colorful fabric for block background

5" square black fabric for mouth interior and pupils

9" square blue fabric, fleece, or fake fur for head and arms

5" square white fabric for eyes and jar bottom

3" square tan print fabric for cookie

5" square pink fabric for jar

Black permanent marker or embroidery thread

Brown embroidery thread (optional)

Tools & Supplies

Tracing paper, #2 pencil, scissors, 8" square tear-away stabilizer, fusible adhesive with paper backing for each shape, iron

Preparing Fusible Appliqué

The appliqué shapes are printed actual size within the block pattern, page 46. You will need to separate the shapes within the block before tracing them onto the paper-side of the fusible adhesive (noting where the shapes overlap). Refer to the General Instructions, pages 10-11, for tips on using the block patterns.

1 Lay a sheet of tracing paper over the block pattern. Using a #2 pencil, carefully trace each shape onto the paper. If you prefer, trace each shape onto separate pieces of paper. Be sure to trace any dashed top-stitching lines.

2 Cut the shapes from the tracing paper and flip them over (reversing the shape) onto the paper-side of the adhesive. Trace the reversed shapes onto the adhesive, again marking any top-stitching placement lines.

3 Cut the shapes from the adhesive, leaving an edge of approximately 1/4" around the solid traced lines.

4 Following the manufacturer's instructions for fusing, iron the cut shapes paper-side up onto the wrong side of the fabric. The color of each shape is shown in the Appliqué Order.

5 Cut the shapes from the newly fused fabric along the marked solid lines of each appliqué. Transfer any top-stitching lines to the right side of the fabric.

Cookie Monster block is a 7 ½" square when sewn.

Fusing the Appliqué Shapes

1 Using the block photograph and pattern (page 46) as a guide for correct placement, remove the paper backing and position the appliqué shapes fabric-side up (in the numbered order) onto the block background square. Dashed lines indicate top-stitching lines. Lightly pencil the word "cookies" onto the jar piece before putting it into place. Note that the background square includes the 1/4" seam allowance.

2 When you are satisfied with the placement, iron the pieces into place. Write over the word "cookies" with a permanent marker, or stitch over it with black embroidery thread.

Satin-Stitch Appliqué (Optional)

1 Refer to the General Instructions, pages 10-11, for tips on satin stitching. Place an 8" piece of tear-away stabilizer under the block, matching all edges.

2 Using a fairly narrow stitch and thread meant for machine appliqué, stitch around the appliqué shapes. Keep your stitch length as short as possible. Stitch over the raw edges of the fused appliqué shapes to cover them. When completed, the stitching should have a smooth "satin" look.

Appliqué Order

1 Black: mouth interior

2 Blue: head

3 White: eyes

4 Black: pupils

5 Blue: arm

6 Tan Print: cookie

7 Pink: jar

8 White: jar bottom

9 Blue: arm

Big Bird

QUILTING WITH THE **MUPPETS**

Materials Needed:

Fabric & Notions

8" square colorful print for block background
3" squares of 6 assorted yellow prints for feathers
3" squares of 3 assorted white prints for brow feathers
5" square red fabric for mouth interior
4" square pink fabric for tongue
9" square yellow fabric for beak
4" square white fabric for eyes
3" square magenta fabric for eyelids
3" square black fabric for pupils
3" square turquoise fabric for eyelines
Yellow embroidery thread (optional)

Tools & Supplies

Tracing paper, #2 pencil, scissors, 8" square tear-away stabilizer
fusible adhesive with paper backing for each shape, iron

Preparing Fusible Appliqué

The appliqué shapes are printed actual size within the block pattern, page 50. You will need to separate the shapes within the block before tracing them onto the paper-side of the fusible adhesive (noting where the shapes overlap). Refer to the General Instructions, pages 10-11, for tips on using the block patterns.

1 Lay a sheet of tracing paper over the block pattern. Using a #2 pencil, carefully trace each shape onto the paper. If you prefer, trace each shape onto separate pieces of paper. Be sure to trace any dashed top-stitching lines.

2 Cut the shapes from the tracing paper and flip them over (reversing the shape) onto the paper-side of the adhesive. Trace the reversed shapes onto the adhesive, again marking any top-stitching placement lines.

3 Cut the shapes from the adhesive, leaving an edge of approximately 1/4" around the solid traced lines.

4 Following the manufacturer's instructions for fusing, iron the cut shapes paper-side up onto the wrong side of the fabric. The color of each shape is shown in the Appliqué Order.

5 Cut the shapes from the newly fused fabric along the marked solid lines of each appliqué. Transfer any top-stitching lines to the right side of the fabric.

T I P S

The instructions for the Big Bird block are for fusible, flat appliqué. Keeping in a yellow color range, select fabrics with interesting patterns and textures.

■ The tall, bouncy feathers that "grow" from the top of Big Bird's head in the original block were made from felt and edged with frayed pieces of embroidery thread. The feathers were attached to the block with short, thin pieces of tubing (yellow thread was inserted through the tubes to add color) and then stitched in place. This technique is best if the quilt is for display only.

■ The original block feathers were first arranged using paper pattern pieces, allowing the designer to experiment with placement. Once the fabric feathers were laid out and appliquéd, they were then outlined with yellow embroidery to unify the block and tie the fabrics together. To simplify the design, you may cut a single piece of yellow fabric following the outline of Big Bird's head, and appliqué it to the background block (top-stitch the feathers for detail). Add the brow feathers before the eyes, and the bouncy feathers at the last.

■ The pattern calls for six different yellow prints for Big Bird's feathers. You may increase the number of prints, if desired.

Big Bird block is a 7 ¹/₂'' square when sewn.

Fusing the Appliqué Shapes

1 Using the block photograph and pattern (page 50) as a guide for correct placement, remove the paper backing and position the appliqué shapes fabric-side up (lay the feathers from the outer edge towards the center, and the features in the numbered order) onto the block background square. Note that the background square includes the 1/4" seam allowance. You may wish to use whole circles for the feathers, trimming the pieces as desired. The eyelines may be appliquéd, as directed, or added using a satin stitch.

2 When you are satisfied with the placement, iron the pieces into place following the manufacturer's instructions. Use several strands of embroidery thread to attach the top feathers to the head as needed.

Satin-Stitch Appliqué (Optional)

1 Refer to the General Instructions, pages 10-11, for tips on satin stitching. Place an 8" piece of tear-away stabilizer under the block, matching all edges.

2 Using a fairly narrow stitch and thread meant for machine appliqué, stitch around the appliqué shapes. Keep your stitch length as short as possible. Stitch over the raw edges of the fused appliqué shapes to cover them. When completed, the stitching should have a smooth "satin" look.

Appliqué Order

| 1 | 2 | 3 | 4 | 5 | 6 |

Yellow Prints: feathers

| 7 | 8 | White Prints: feathers

| 9 | Red: mouth interior

| 10 | 13 | Magenta: tongue, eyelids

| 11 | Yellow: beak

| 12 | White: eyes

| 14 | Black: pupils

| 15 | Turquoise: eyelines

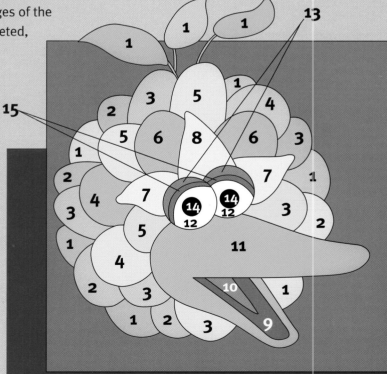

Kermit the Frog

Materials Needed:

Fabric & Notions

8" square colorful fabric for block background
10" square green fabric for arm, body, and face
4" square red fabric for mouth interior
3" square pink fabric for tongue
4" square white fabric for eyes
3" square black fabric for pupils
8" square light green fabric for collar

Tools & Supplies

Tracing paper, #2 pencil, scissors, 8" square tear-away stabilizer, fusible adhesive with paper backing for each shape, iron

Preparing Fusible Appliqué

The appliqué shapes are printed actual size within the block pattern, page 54. You will need to separate the shapes within the block before tracing them onto the paper-side of the fusible adhesive (noting where the shapes overlap). Refer to the General Instructions, pages 10-11, for tips on using the block patterns.

1 Lay a sheet of tracing paper over the block pattern. Using a #2 pencil, carefully trace each shape onto the paper. If you prefer, trace each shape onto separate pieces of paper. Be sure to trace any dashed top-stitching lines.

2 Cut the shapes from the tracing paper and flip them over (reversing the shape) onto the paper-side of the adhesive. Trace the reversed shapes onto the adhesive, again marking any top-stitching placement lines.

3 Cut the shapes from the adhesive, leaving an edge of approximately $1/4$" around the solid traced lines.

4 Following the manufacturer's instructions for fusing, iron the cut shapes paper-side up onto the wrong side of the fabric. The color of each shape is shown in the Appliqué Order.

5 Cut the shapes from the newly fused fabric along the marked solid lines of each appliqué. Transfer any top-stitching lines to the right side of the fabric.

T I P S

The instructions given for the Kermit block are for fusible flat appliqué. If you wish to add dimension to your block with sculpted foam or other elements, you will need to add fabric accordingly.

■ *The original Kermit block was made with ultra-suede fabric to avoid having to hem the collar or the fingers.*

■ *Instead of using a single piece of patterned fabric for the background block, you can sew together strips of different fabrics to create a colorful collage. Be sure to use a piece of solid fabric behind Kermit's hand if you wish to add a letter or number.*

Kermit block is a 7 ¹/2" square when sewn.

Fusing the Appliqué Shapes

1 Using the block photograph and pattern (page 54) as a guide for correct placement, remove the paper backing and position the appliqué shapes fabric-side up (in the numbered order) onto the block background square. Dashed lines indicate top-stitching lines. Note that the background square includes the 1/4" seam allowance.

2 When you are satisfied with the placement, iron the pieces into place following the manufacturer's instructions.

Satin-Stitch Appliqué (Optional)·

1 Refer to the General Instructions, pages 10-11, for tips on satin stitching. Place an 8" piece of tear-away stabilizer under the block, matching all edges.

2 Using a narrow stitch and thread meant for machine appliqué, stitch around the appliqué shapes. Keep your stitch length as short as possible. Stitch over the raw edges of the fused appliqué shapes to cover them. When completed, the stitching should have a smooth "satin" look.

Appliqué Order

1	**2**	**3**	Green: arm, body, face
4			Red: mouth interior
5			Pink: tongue
6			White: eyes
7			Black: pupils
8			Light Green: collar

Bert and Bernice

Materials Needed:

Fabric & Notion

8" square colorful print for block background
5" square striped fabric for shirt
9" square white fabric for shirt and eyes
9" square yellow fabric for head, ear, and hand
6" square red fabric for Bert's mouth interior
7" square black fabric for eyebrows, pupils, Bernice's beak and eye
5" square black fabric, fleece, or fake fur for hair
4" square pink fabric for tongue
4" square orange fabric for nose
3" square gray print fabric for Bernice's body
Silver embroidery thread or soutache for paperclip

Tools & Supplies

Tracing paper, #2 pencil, scissors, 8" square tear-away stabilizer, fusible adhesive with paper backing for each shape, iron

Preparing Fusible Appliqué

The appliqué shapes are printed actual size within the block pattern, page 58. You will need to separate the shapes within the block before tracing them onto the paper-side of the fusible adhesive (noting where the shapes overlap). Refer to the General Instructions, pages 10-11, for tips on using the block patterns.

1 Lay a sheet of tracing paper over the block pattern. Using a #2 pencil, carefully trace each shape onto the paper. If you prefer, trace each shape onto separate pieces of paper. Be sure to trace any dashed top-stitching lines.

2 Cut the shapes from the tracing paper and flip them over (reversing the shape) onto the paper-side of the adhesive. Trace the reversed shapes onto the adhesive, again marking any top-stitching placement lines.

3 Cut the shapes from the adhesive, leaving an edge of approximately 1/4" around the solid traced lines.

4 Following the manufacturer's instructions for fusing, iron the cut shapes paper-side up onto the wrong side of the fabric. The color of each shape is shown in the Appliqué Order.

5 Cut the shapes from the newly fused fabric along the marked solid lines of each appliqué. Transfer any top-stitching lines to the right side of the fabric.

T I P S

The instructions for the Bert block are for fusible, flat appliqué.

■ If desired, you may cut and appliqué a block letter "B" to the background block, referring to the photograph for placement.

■ If you select a stripe for Bert's shirt, you may wish to piece it to match the direction of the stripes on the body and arm of the shirt, as shown.

■ Buttons may be substituted for Bert's pupils and Bernice's eye. If the quilt is for a small child, however, the eyes should be appliquéd or embroidered. Stitch Bernice's eye, then sew a small, lighter-colored bead into the center of the stitch for the highlight in the eye.

■ You may add the paper clip using silver embroidery thread in a narrow satin stitch, or by stitching silver soutache in a paper clip shape.

■ Bert's hair can be applied using fake fur. For sewing directions, see pages 10-11.

Bert block is a 7 ¹/₂" square when sewn.

Fusing the Appliqué Shapes

1 Using the block photograph and pattern (page 58) as a guide for correct placement, remove the paper backing and position the appliqué shapes fabric side up (in the numbered order) onto the block background square. Dashed lines indicate top-stitching lines. Note that the background square includes the 1/4" seam allowance.

2 When you are satisfied with the placement, iron the pieces into place following the manufacturer's instructions.

Satin-Stitch Appliqué (Optional)

1 Refer to the General Instructions, pages 10-11, for tips on satin stitching. Place an 8" piece of tear-away stabilizer under block, matching all edges.

2 Using a narrow stitch and thread meant for machine appliqué, stitch around the appliqué shapes. Keep your stitch length as short as possible. Stitch over the raw edges of the fused appliqué shapes to cover them. When completed, the stitching should have a smooth "satin" look.

Appliqué Order

1 Stripe: shirt

2 **4** **7** White: shirt, eyes

3 **11** **18** Yellow: head, ear, hand

5 Red: mouth interior

6 Pink: tongue

8 **9** **12** Black: pupils, eyebrow, hair

10 Orange: nose

13 **14** Gray print: Bernice's body, wing

15 Silver: paperclip

16 **17** Black: Bernice's beak, eye

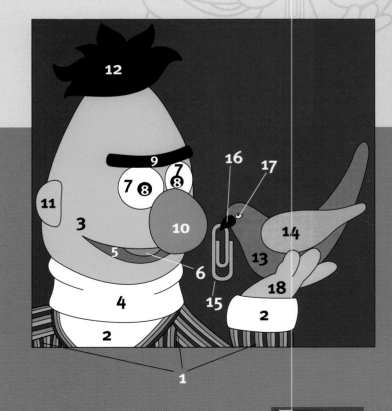

Oscar the Grouch

Materials Needed:

Fabric & Notions

8" square brick print fabric for block background, see Tips

6" square metallic silver print fabric for trashcan

9" square green fabric, fleece, or fake fur for face and body

6" square black fabric for mouth interior and pupils

4" square pinkish brown fabric for tongue

4" square white fabric for eyes

6" square brown fabric, fleece, or fake fur for eyebrows

Tools & Supplies

Tracing paper, #2 pencil, scissors, 8" square tear-away stabilizer, fusible adhesive with paper backing for each shape, iron

Preparing Fusible Appliqué

The appliqué shapes are printed actual size within the block pattern, page 62. You will need to separate the shapes within the block before tracing them onto the paper-side of the fusible adhesive (noting where the shapes overlap). Refer to the General Instructions, pages 10-11, for tips on using the block patterns.

1 Lay a sheet of tracing paper over the block pattern. Using a #2 pencil, carefully trace each shape onto the paper. If you prefer, trace each shape onto separate pieces of paper. Be sure to trace any dashed top-stitching lines.

2 Cut the shapes from the tracing paper and flip them over (reversing the shape) onto the paper-side of the adhesive. Trace the reversed shapes onto the adhesive, again marking any top-stitching placement lines.

3 Cut the shapes from the adhesive, leaving an edge of approximately 1/4" around the solid traced lines.

4 Following the manufacturer's instructions for fusing, iron the cut shapes paper-side up onto the wrong side of the fabric. The color of each shape is shown in the Appliqué Order.

5 Cut the shapes from the newly fused fabric along the marked solid lines of each appliqué. Transfer any top-stitching lines to the right side of the fabric.

T I P S

The original Oscar the Grouch block was made with actual fabrics used for the Muppet. The instructions given for the block are for fusible, flat appliqué. If you choose to use additional materials to add dimension, you will need to increase the fabric amounts accordingly.

▪ If you are unable to find a brick-patterned print, you may create the bricks yourself. Simply cut brick-sized rectangles from an 8" square of dark red fabric, and appliqué them onto an 8" square of gray fabric.

▪ Before you appliqué the trash can to the background block, be sure to test a scrap of the fabric with an iron. Some metallic fabrics tend to dull when heat is applied— if your scrap loses its metallic finish upon ironing, you may want to stitch it in place instead. Some woven fabrics, such as "lurex," fare better under the iron.

Oscar the Grouch block is a 7 $\frac{1}{2}$" square when sewn.

Fusing the Appliqué Shapes

1 Using the block photograph and pattern (page 62) as a guide for correct placement, remove the paper backing and position the appliqué shapes fabric-side up (in the numbered order) onto the block background square. Dashed lines indicate top-stitching lines. Note that the background square includes the 1/4" seam allowance.

2 When you are satisfied with the placement, fuse the pieces into place following the manufacturer's instructions.

Satin-Stitch Appliqué (Optional)

1 Refer to the General Instructions, pages 10-11, for tips on satin stitching. Place an 8" piece of tear-away stabilizer under block, matching all edges.

2 Using a fairly narrow stitch and thread meant for machine appliqué, stitch around the appliqué shapes. Keep your stitch length as short as possible. Stitch over the raw edges of the fused appliqué shapes to cover them. When completed, the stitching should have a smooth "satin" look.

Appliqué Order

1 Silver: trash can

2 Green: face, body

3 **6** Black: mouth interior, pupils

4 Pinkish Brown: tongue

5 White: eyes

7 Brown: eyebrows

8 **9** Green: hands, finger

Elmo

Materials Needed:

Fabric & Notions
8" square colorful print for block background
12" square red fabric for body, hands, and face
6" square black fabric for mouth interior and pupils
4" square white fabric for eyes
4" square orange fabric for nose

Tools & Supplies
Tracing paper, #2 pencil, scissors, 8" square tear-away stabilizer, fusible adhesive with paper backing for each shape, iron

Preparing Fusible Appliqué
The appliqué shapes are printed actual size within the block pattern, page 66. You will need to separate the shapes within the block before tracing them onto the paper-side of the fusible adhesive (noting where the shapes overlap). Refer to the General Instructions, pages 10-11, for tips on using the block patterns.

1 Lay a sheet of tracing paper over the block pattern. Using a #2 pencil, carefully trace each shape onto the paper. If you prefer, trace each shape onto separate pieces of paper. Be sure to trace any dashed top-stitching lines.

2 Cut the shapes from the tracing paper and flip them over (reversing the shape) onto the paper-side of the adhesive. Trace the reversed shapes onto the adhesive, again marking any top-stitching placement lines.

3 Cut the shapes from the adhesive, leaving an edge of approximately 1/4" around the solid traced lines.

4 Following the manufacturer's instructions for fusing, iron the cut shapes paper-side up onto the wrong side of the fabric. The color of each shape is shown in the Appliqué Order.

5 Cut the shapes from the newly fused fabric along the marked solid lines of each appliqué. Transfer any top-stitching lines to the right side of the fabric.

T I P S

The instructions given for the Elmo block are for fusible, flat appliqué. If you choose to use fake fur to duplicate Elmo's characteristic fuzziness, refer to the instructions on page 10-11.

Elmo block is a 7 $^1/_2$" square when sewn

Fusing the Appliqué Shapes

1 Using the block photograph and pattern (page 66) as a guide for correct placement, remove the paper backing and position the appliqué shapes fabric-side up (in the numbered order) onto the block background square. Dashed lines indicate where pieces should overlap. Note that the background square includes the 1/4" seam allowance.

2 When you are satisfied with the placement, iron the pieces into place following the manufacturer's instructions.

Satin-Stitch Appliqué (Optional)

1 Refer to the General Instructions, pages 10-11, for tips on satin stitching. Place an 8" piece of tear-away stabilizer under block, matching all edges.

2 Using a fairly narrow stitch and thread meant for machine appliqué, stitch around the appliqué shapes. Keep your stitch length as short as possible. Stitch over the raw edges of the fused appliqué shapes to cover them. When completed, the stitching should have a smooth "satin" look.

Appliqué Order

1 **2** **3** Red: body, hands, face

4 **6** Black: mouth interior, pupils

5 White: eyes

7 Orange: nose

Grover

SUPERHEROS

QUILTING WITH THE **MUPPETS**

Materials Needed:

Fabric & Notions

8" square colorful print fabric for block background
8" square red print fabric for book jacket
9" square blue print fabric for face and hands
5" square white fabric for book pages and eyes
6" square dusty rose fabric for lip
3" square black fabric for pupils
5" square magenta fabric for nose
Black embroidery thread to outline shapes, see Tips (optional)
Tan embroidery thread to stitch title of Grover's book, see Tips

Tools & Supplies

Tracing paper, #2 pencil, scissors, 8" square tear-away stabilizer, fusible adhesive with paper backing for each shape, iron

Preparing Fusible Appliqué

The appliqué shapes are printed actual size within the block pattern, page 70. You will need to separate the shapes within the block before tracing them onto the paper-side of the fusible adhesive (noting where the shapes overlap). Refer to the General Instructions, pages 10-11, for tips on using the block patterns.

1 Lay a sheet of tracing paper over the block pattern. Using a #2 pencil, carefully trace each shape onto the paper. If you prefer, trace each shape onto separate pieces of paper. Be sure to trace any dashed top-stitching lines.

2 Cut the shapes from the tracing paper and flip them over (reversing the shape) onto the paper-side of the adhesive. Trace the reversed shapes onto the adhesive, again marking any top-stitching placement lines.

3 Cut the shapes from the adhesive, leaving an edge of approximately $1/4$" around the solid traced lines.

4 Following the manufacturer's instructions for fusing, iron the cut shapes paper-side up onto the wrong side of the fabric. The color of each shape is shown in the Appliqué Order.

5 Cut the shapes from the newly fused fabric along the marked solid lines of each appliqué. Transfer any top-stitching lines to the right side of the fabric.

T I P S

The instructions given for the Grover block are for fusible, flat appliqué. You may choose print fabrics to give the head and body more interest. Black top-stitching around the shapes will add definition.

■ *Stitch the book title "Superheros" to the spine of the book using embroidery thread, or add the title with a permanent marker in a dark or metallic color.*

■ *Stitch with black thread along the dashed lines on the book pages to define the separation of the pages. You can increase the amount of pages by stitching more lines, as desired.*

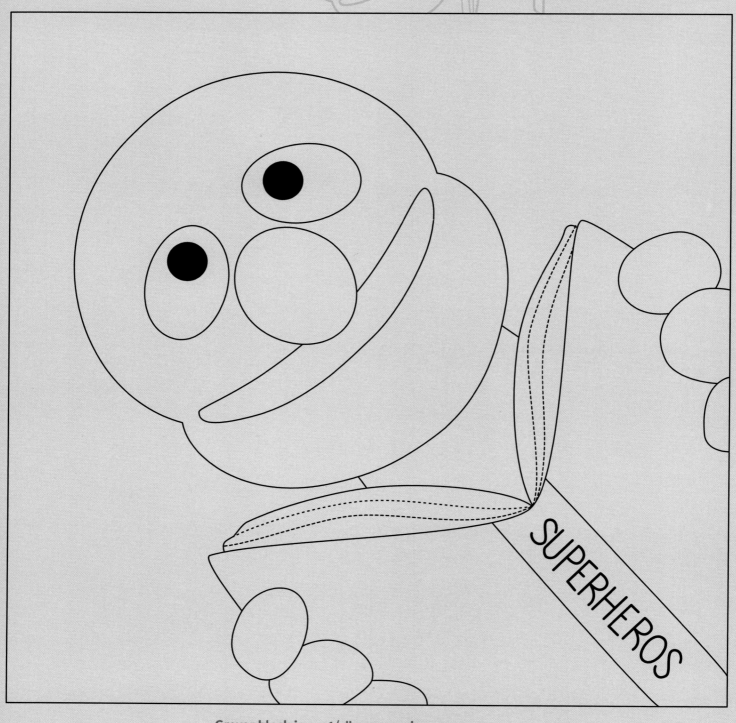

Grover block is a 7 ½" square when sewn.

QUILTING WITH THE **MUPPETS**

Fusing the Appliqué Shapes

1 Using the block photograph and pattern (page 70) as a guide for correct placement, remove the paper backing and position all appliqué shapes (in the numbered order) onto the block background square. Dashed lines indicate top-stitching lines. Note that the background square includes the $1/4$" seam allowance.

2 When you are satisfied with the placement, fuse the pieces into place following the manufacturer's instructions.

Satin-Stitch Appliqué (Optional)

1 Refer to the General Instructions, pages 10-11, for tips on satin stitching. Place an 8" piece of tear-away stabilizer under block, matching all edges.

2 Using a fairly narrow stitch and thread meant for machine appliqué, stitch around the appliqué shapes. Keep your stitch length as short as possible. Stitch over the raw edges of the fused appliqué shapes to cover them. When completed, the stitching should have a smooth "satin" look.

Appliqué Order

1 **2**	Red Print: book jacket, book spine
3 **5**	Blue Print: face, neck, hands
4 **7**	White: book pages, eyes
6	Red: lip
8	Black: pupils
9	Magenta: nose

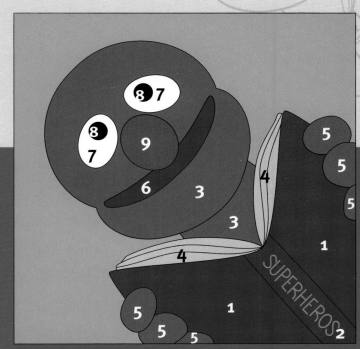

Muppet Friendship Quilts: Preface

For over 30 years the Muppet Workshop has occupied several different buildings within a few blocks in Manhattan. Scores of people have worked in the Workshop, for periods ranging from two weeks to over two decades. As in any company, people have married, had children, marked anniversaries and, unfortunately, passed away. The Jim Henson Company's Muppet Workshop has commemorated many of these occasions by creating friendship quilts.

To me, this is the real story of this book. We are a group of people with various levels of sewing skills and knowledge of quilting, working together to turn out something beautiful and full of love.

Our first quilt came on the heels of my own introduction to quilting, just after my mother's death. An avid sewer, she died without seeing any of her quilt tops quilted. My goal was to have these pieces finished, which eventually led me to designing tops of my own. My new interest proved to be a springboard for our first Muppet friendship quilt. When co-worker Mary Strieff made the extraordinary decision to become a single mother 15 years ago, my colleagues and I realized that her momentous choice required a fitting gift.

The 32 quilts we have made so far are the embodiment of the quintessential friendship quilt: each is a quilt made for friends by friends. Some of the contributors, like Connie Peterson, have been quilting for over 25 years. Others, like those in administration or the electro-mechanical department, can barely sew. Nonetheless, everyone who has wanted to make a quilt square has been able to. Some of the most beautiful quilt squares were created by first-time quilters. Their squares often retold a story or personal moment that related to the recipient.

Except for the Muppet banner, these quilts were made on our own time and paid for by us, the employees. They were truly collaborative efforts—those people who were unable to make a square often contributed fabric or money. Perhaps the single most gratifying quilt was the one we made to celebrate the 30th anniversary of "Sesame Street." It raised $36,000 at an auction for several children's charities.

Over the years, we agreed that no one here had the time to do the quilting. Instead we decided to take up a collection and hire an expert quilter to do it. Our first tops were quilted by Katie Miller. When she passed away we found other quilters including Barbara Bullis and then Olivia Klaus, who has done the majority of the work. We are exceedingly grateful to these women for their part in creating these quilts. Without them we would have only friendship quilt tops!

Anyone with a basic knowledge of quiltmaking can organize a friendship quilt. It is my hope that this book will inspire you to commemorate an important event with a friendship quilt, or create a quilt for your favorite charity. When we began, no one imagined that we would eventually turn out this incredible body of work. We all look forward to seeing what we will create in the years to come.

— STEPHEN ROTONDARO
"Sesame Street" Muppet Supervisor

BABY QUILT FOR MARY STREIFF'S SON JONATHAN

Mary Streiff, a costumer, was the first person in the Workshop to receive a friendship baby quilt. Her quilt features a block made by Caroly Wilcox that pictures hearts and a pig, because Mary collects pigs. The hearts also turned out to be a lovely, though accidental, recurring theme throughout the quilt. The block that says "baby" is by Polly Smith and was inspired by the graffiti on New York's subways. Susie Cox made the square of A Mother and Her Child.

A Pig Jumping Over Hearts

A Mother and Her Child

"*The baby quilt presented to me on Memorial Day, 1987, represented not only all the close friends I had made during my years working at Henson Associates, but also the journey ahead as a single mother by choice. The family of friends and associates at one of the most creative and supportive companies in the world totally surprised me with this quilt at my baby shower. I still remember gasping, and then the tears of joy, when I realized what everyone had done. This was the very first in a long line of beautiful, meaningful, and extraordinary quilts, honoring births, deaths, retirements and other landmark events of our friends and family at the Muppets.*"

— MARY STRIEFF

"*Mary likes pigs and had a small collection of cookie jars with pigs on them, so I thought 'pig' when I learned she was due for a quilt. The color scheme was blue, yellow, and white, so I made a patchwork yellow pig. First I just sewed a crazy scrap 'blob,' ironed it, then transferred the pig outline onto the blob. I cut outside the outline shape, leaving a $1/4$" seam, snipped to the outline to aid in turning the seam under, pinned it in place, and started stitching it down, removing or adding pins as needed. The horizontal pig wouldn't fill a whole square, so I added a row of hearts.*"

— CAROLY WILCOX

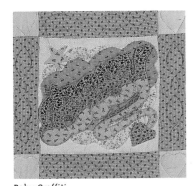

Baby Graffiti

Flowers

Train

RETIREMENT QUILT FOR CAROLY WILCOX

Caroly Wilcox was in charge of puppet building for Sesame Street for many years. The quilt made for her retirement features many characters, some made by the puppeteers who perform them (Marty Robinson's Snuffy, Pam Arciero's Grudgetta) or by the builders who make the puppets for Sesame Street (Sheep by Peter MacKennan, Forgetful Jones by Richard Termine, Martians by Kip Rathke). Others depict characters that Caroly made, like Scred from "Saturday Night Live" or Earl the Dragon flashing the peace sign. Several blocks depict aspects of her life outside work: a portrait of her house, irises in her garden, the deer that nibble at the garden, and a piano for her love of music. The embroidered Big Bird feather was done by Janice Herbert, who was the chief feather-sorter for several years. The middle block in the bottom row is by Jason Weber—it contains 700 separate pieces. The Bus Full of Snuffies was made by Christine Moyes, using French knots to replicate the Snuffies' fur. Caroly sometimes played the school bus driver on the show.

Himalayas

Snuffy

"My block for Caroly was done to commemorate our individual journeys to Asia which overlapped in Nepal. The overlap was an odd coincidence so we planned to meet while there. We flew to Mt. Everest and back since neither of us had an itinerary that would accommodate a trek to the legendary mountain. The quilt block depicts the range of lights and darks of the Himalayas rising up from the valley floor to the sky. The mountains are so high that parts often seem to disappear in the distance. It's possible to mistake the peaks for clouds if you don't look carefully.

The writing is 'Namaste,' which is a commonly used Nepali greeting. The surround of maroon- and saffron-colored stitching is symbolic of robes worn by the Buddhist monks at the temples in Nepal."

— JULIE ZOBEL

"I'd been performing Snuffleupagus for a number of years before Caroly retired, so I depicted myself peeking out and waving to her from inside Snuffy's mouth (as is actually possible). Caroly's reaction was that she recalled being in the front end of Snuffy only a few times . . . I didn't have the heart to tell her it was me, not her, in the quilt . . . till now"

— MARTY ROBINSON

C is for Caroly

Forgetful Jones and Buster

"The quilt the Muppet designers and performers made for me left me speechless and thrilled. It has such history, humor, vitality, skill, and love in it. WOW!"

— CAROLY WILCOX

"The C is for Caroly square was made for Caroly's retirement. The letter C is brought to you by "Sesame Street," which was my very first job! Caroly hired me. I was so in awe when on the "Sesame Street" set for the first time. I had studied Jim Henson in my course work at the University of Connecticut, pursuing a degree in puppetry. I remember the first time I saw Jim and Frank performing Bert and Ernie; it was so thrilling. Caroly and the Jim Henson Workshop made that moment possible for me."

— JAN ROSENTHAL STEFURA

Piano

Honkers

Earl the Dragon

NAMES PROJECT PANEL FOR RICHARD HUNT

Richard Hunt was a fabulous, talented, joyous puppeteer and friend. When the decision was made to create a panel for the NAMES Project AIDS quilt for him, the artists at the Workshop wanted it to reflect all that his Muppet characters had given them and the world. The most difficult and unique aspect of making this quilt was knowing that Richard would never see it. Perhaps the act of creating the panel was the quilters' way of dealing with that fact.

Beaker

"I chose to do Beaker for Richard's quilt because he was one of my favorite "Muppet Show" characters and, of course, Richard performed him. I specifically chose Beaker singing "Feelings" because it was a favorite Richard/Beaker moment. This quilt meant a lot to me. Hopefully, it conveyed to the world how special Richard was to us and just a bit of what he brought to the world; how much he actually contributed really can't be measured."
— ROLLIE KREWSON

Belmont

Forgetful Jones

"I chose to make a square of Forgetful Jones (a gentle cowboy who doesn't realize he can't remember much of anything). I depicted Forgetful peering through a heart-shaped hole. To replicate him in a realistic way, I used fabrics similar to those that are used to make the actual puppet. Forgetful Jones, a 'Sesame Street' character, brought out more of the simple, sweet side of Richard, in the midst of some of his other more outrageous characters."

— LAURENT LINN

"Belmont was a Muppet character that I designed and created for a Jim Henson Christmas television special, 'The Christmas Toy.' Richard Hunt was the brilliant puppeteer who performed this dopey, yet ultimately heroic, character. I consider it one of my favorite and most successful characters in my 22-year career in the Muppet Workshop.

The character was appliquéd onto a pieced fabric background. Shapes were then enhanced with embroidery around the edges. The word 'BELMONT' is embroidered using a chain stitch. Buttons were used for the wheels and the handle near the horse's mane.

I think that all of the quilt squares in the Richard Hunt memorial quilt represent his genius, and they add up to an amazing art piece. I am so proud to have been a friend of his and among the company of artists who contributed to this quilt."

— ED CHRISTIE

Richard Hunt Caricature

"Richard was always poking fun at me and I would invariably return the favor visually. This is one of many caricatures I drew of Richard during our friendship. For this block, I used fabric paint to draw on a piece of one of his old T-shirts. We both shared the belief that good-natured teasing was an act of love — we teased each other a lot!"

— DON REARDON

Two-Headed Monster

"I felt very fortunate to be able to represent the Two-Headed Monster on this quilt. Richard was an extraordinary performer with a great sense of humor, and this character represented his humor at its boisterous best. Along with Beaker, it's among my favorite characters. Since I spent six seasons on the 'Sesame Street' staff, it seemed appropriate that I chose a 'Sesame Street' character (in this case, maybe characters). The square was simple, made with a fur-fabric, feather appliqué, and embroidery. I used fabric pulled from the actual puppet material drawers, staying close to what I used as a puppet builder on the show."

— PETER MACKENNAN

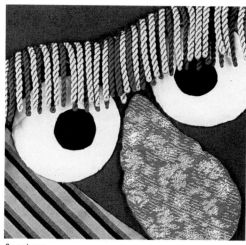

Sweetums

"This was one of the first quilt squares that I ever made. I wanted this monster to be an abstract representation of the Muppet monster Sweetums that was performed by Richard Hunt. Sweetums has a big orange nose and brown shaggy fur. He is big and lumbering and has a very sweet personality. Sweetums and Robin the Frog, Kermit's nephew, make a wonderfully unusual singing couple (as Robin fits inside the palm of Sweetums's hand). I loved Richard's Sweetums. My brother John took on the part of Sweetums after Richard died—it's nice to know that the character that Richard created lives on."

— CHERYL HENSON

Richard Hunt Name

"My colors for this block were intentional. I chose yellow for the star because of the star that Richard was, he was constantly in motion. He was full of happiness, fun, playfulness, and he had a truly gregarious spirit. For his name I chose red because it represents fire, blood, heart, and passion, everything that Richard stood for. I picked corduroy as my medium because with all that Richard possessed, he was down to earth and knew the meaning of friendship."

— BARBARA S. DAVIS

BABY QUILT FOR RICHARD TERMINE'S SON COLIN

Richard Termine started as a puppet builder in the Workshop, and is a talented photographer who has done set photography for "Sesame Street" for years. Richard's quilt has two characters that he built for "Sesame Street": Wolfgang the Seal and Placido Flamingo. Rubber Duckie was included because he's a favorite on "Sesame Street," and seemed a good choice for a baby's quilt. Grundgetta and Telly Monster were created by their respective "Sesame Street" puppeteers, Pam Arciero and Marty Robinson. The Ohio Star block was in honor of the fact that Richard lived in Ohio at the time.

Telly Monster

"The square is designed after a photo that Richard took of me with my character Telly Monster. Telly is looking directly at the viewer and seems really scared. I left myself out—otherwise, it might have been really scary. The background is TV static."
— MARTY ROBINSON

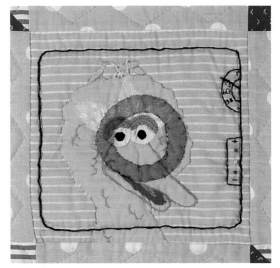

Big Bird

"It would be hard to count the number of times Richard has looked at Big Bird through his camera lens. So for Richard's quilt I decided to represent Big Bird in a special way—through a viewfinder. I began the square by sewing together an image of Big Bird's face using fabrics that would tie in with the colors and textures chosen for the overall quilt. I then used embroidery thread to stitch a line replicating what we might see in the viewfinder: a light meter and an aperture gauge. I added a ring of sheer black netting in the center to suggest the focus ring. What I like best about this square is that one has to think about it and know Richard to understand what it means. It takes an internationally-known character and makes him personal."
— LAURENT LINN

Big Bird and Barkley

"Big Bird and Barkley looking at Mt. Fuji refers to the fact that Richard was among those who went to Japan to shoot the 'Big Bird in Japan' special."
— MARK ZESZOTEK

BABY QUILT FOR ROBERTA HAMELIN'S SON RYAN

Roberta Hamelin worked at the Workshop creating body costumes for stage show productions. Ann Marie Holdgruen, a Muppet builder, decided to make a Spools of Thread block since Roberta spent three summers stitching fast and furiously. Ed Christie, who currently runs the Workshop, made a Shoofly block with one beautiful fly embroidered on it. Lisa Howard created the Pull-Toy block. The Elephant Island block, by Christine Moyes, was inspired by a wonderful elephant-print fabric. The quilt is very special in Roberta's family, and hangs on the wall in Ryan's bedroom. After receiving the quilt, Roberta became so inspired by her friend Stephen Rotandaro's quilt projects that she later headed up a quilt project at her son's school that raised nearly $4,000.

Elephant Island

BABY QUILT FOR TOM NEWBY'S SON JESSE

Tom's quilt has an Elvis theme, so Ed Christie made a signature insect square called Blue Suede Shoofly based on the traditional Shoofly pattern. Ed used blue ultrasuede for one of the fabrics, inserted grommets and laces, and embroidered a tiny fly on the block. Another block, Don't Bee Cruel, has a large bee with the international symbol for "no" (circle with a slash) embroidered as a large-scale chain stitch over the insect.

Blue Christmas

"The quilt square I made for Tom Newby and his wife, Connie, was based on their Christmas card from some years before. It shows their house in the wintertime. When we decided on the Elvis theme for Tom's quilt, I worked from the card design to make a 'Blue Christmas' square. It was an easy choice."
— STEPHEN ROTONDARO

BABY QUILT FOR JOE HENDERSON'S DAUGHTER SARAH

Joe's quilt features Chinese themes and the characters for "longevity" and "double happiness." It was made in honor of his adoption of a Chinese baby girl. The quilt features a couple of extraordinary blocks, one of a Chinese lion done in reverse appliqué by Jason Weber, and one of a crane which was appliquéd and beautifully embroidered by David Roberts. It also features a block by Barbara Davis of the little girl's American name, Sarah.

Big Bird

Crane

"My choice of a crane was based on the use of this bird as a symbol of wishes for a long life in Chinese and other East Asian cultures. The actual design of the motif is based on elements found embroidered on Imperial robes from the Forbidden City. I attempted to imitate the character of Far Eastern embroideries through the types and direction of the stitches."

— DAVID ROBERTS

"I made Big Bird because he's my favorite character, and because Joe's daughter Sarah was being adopted from China, where Big Bird is as loved as he is in the USA. I wanted to use a character that represents both of the cultures to which Sarah belongs. I kept the design of Big Bird simple. I knew that my block would be the only square depicting a Muppet character, and I didn't want it to be more complex than the other squares. In order to better blend the block with the rest of the quilt, I used some fabrics from other blocks. (Happily, Big Bird's colors work quite well within the chosen color scheme.) I was hoping for the square to have a somewhat abstract quality so that it didn't immediately pop out. Big Bird should be a very happy discovery as one looks at the details of the quilt."

— LAURENT LINN

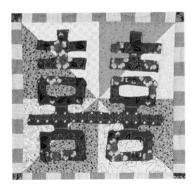

Double Happiness

Longevity

Lion

BABY QUILT FOR PAUL ANDREJCO'S DAUGHTER JANE

The quilt for Paul Andrejco features characters designed by him and his wife. Paul designed the characters for the series "Bear in the Big Blue House." The show is represented in the quilt by squares of Tutter the mouse (by Kip Rathke), Shadow (by Barbara Davis), Ray (by Mary Brehmer), and Bear (by Christine Moyes). Paul's wife Shari is a children's book illustrator—the child riding a horse (by Rollie Krewson) and the border design are both inspired by her illustrations.

Bear

Horse

"The Bear block by Christine Moyes is one of the most elaborate blocks, showing a door flanked by brass lamps. It's the door to the set of 'Bear in the Big Blue House.' If you open the door, Bear is embroidered on the inside. Christine was one of the builders of the Bear character, and worked for two seasons on the set of the show."
— C O N N I E   P E T E R S O N

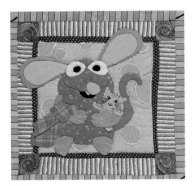

Tutter

Cat Sleeping Among the Flowers

Milk Carton Cow

BABY QUILT FOR PAM ARCIERO'S SON NICHOLAS

Pam didn't know about the friendship quilts until she was presented with one for the birth of her son. She was surpised and thrilled. What she finds particularly wonderful is the key on the back of the quilt with the names of the people who love her enough to sew a square for her. The quilt hangs outside her son's bedroom, and he can see it when he lies in bed. Pam smiles everytime she passes it, as a square or two always stands out. It brings Pam great joy, and she feels deeply honored to have received the quilt.

Telly Monster

"Pam is my right-hand partner in Telly Monster, and we used to do a lot of reporter bits. Here, Telly is interviewing a trash can that I always imagined held a camera-shy Oscar or Grundgetta—much easier for my limited sewing skills to leave Grouches to the imagination. I worked a personal message to Pam into the stitching around Telly."
— MARTY ROBINSON

BABY QUILT FOR CARMEN OSBAHR'S SON ALEXANDER

As a child growing up in Mexico City, Carmen Osbahr's dream was to someday work as a puppeteer for the Jim Henson Company. When she first arrived in the United States, Carmen spoke almost no English but was determined to follow her dream. Twelve years, a lot of work, and countless language lessons later, Carmen is a veteran performer on "Sesame Street." Carmen's character Rosita, the first Latino Muppet regular on the American version of "Sesame Street," is depicted in the quilt. A truly international family, Carmen and her British husband Neil live in Connecticut with their son Alexander, and their little dog Dexter (look for him in the quilt, too).

Finger Puppet Family

"I made the portrait puppets [of Carmen's family] out of felt, with small details of felt, embroidery, and beads. The theater backdrop is simply a piece of fabric cut from Sesame Street sheets that feature Rosita in a fairy tale theme. The curtains were made with gathered fabric and bugle beads, and the stage was made with fabric and buttons. I made the theater so that the finger puppets could be removed and played with, then buttoned back into place on the stage. This way the quilt square is much more than purely visual."

—LAURENT LINN

BABY QUILT FOR LAUREN ATTINELLO'S SON BENJAMIN

Lauren first came to the company working for Connie Peterson on *Sesame Street Live*. The simple geometric blocks on Lauren's quilt were made by Marcia Peterson (Connie's sister) who participated in a quilting bee with Lauren. Some of the fabrics in the blocks were purchased in Japan when Mark Zeszotek was there for a Big Bird television special. The block depicting Lauren drawing Kermit rock climbing (by Caroly Wilcox) refers to Lauren's career change from Muppet builder to art director, and her interest in rock climbing at the time.

Bug

"I began using the insect as a subject for quilting as a reaction to what I call 'nice' themes usually found on quilts. I wanted to find a motif that is abhorred by many and put it in a context where it is beloved by all. I wanted to portray the insect as realistically as possible, but not as a cutesified object. I wanted to represent its complex anatomy as accurately as possible within the standards of the quilting medium: enhancing it with common decorative methods such as adding buttons and embroidery. In effect, making the critter quite cherished and accepted within our home, even on our bed!"
— ED CHRISTIE

Lauren and Kermit

"I chose this subject because Lauren had worked in the Muppet Workshop and had meticulously re-created many Kermits for a Muppet movie. She is also a fine illustrator, so I depicted her drawing Kermit."
— CAROLY WILCOX

Baby

"Stephen [Rotondaro] sewed my wedding dress with impeccable skill, so his blocks are very special to me. His 'Baby' block incorporates embroidery from an old pillowcase."
— LAUREN ATTINELLO

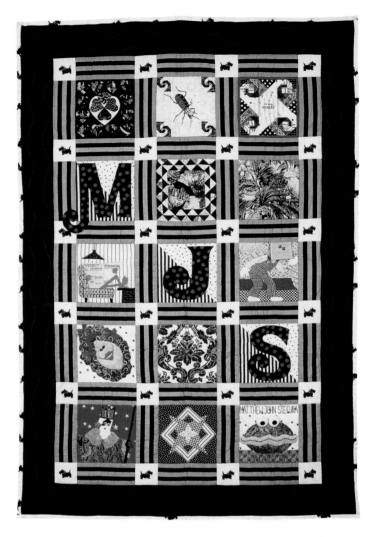

BABY QUILT FOR JAN ROSENTHAL STEFURA'S SON MATTHEW

The black and white color scheme of Jan Rosenthal Stefura's quilt was inspired by the pencil drawings by her artist husband Michael. Jan made lots of puppets for "The Muppet Show," including Lottie Lemon and her Singing Wig, plus lots of clams. The other characters are some she designed before coming to the Muppets. Ed Christie contributed an insect square to this quilt, just as in the quilts for Tom Newby and Lauren Attinello.

Kermit Reading Newspaper

"Black and white and red all over just seemed to suggest a newspaper. Kermit was the perfect choice to read it... Jan used clean lines and a wonderful modern look in her work, so I went in that direction, keeping it graphic by using simple shapes."

— JANE GOOTNICK

Newspaper Man

"When I first started working at Sesame Street, I rode the subway to work. One day there was a man sitting across from me reading a newspaper... Nothing unusual in that, except that he was watching me through two holes ripped in the newspaper. I told Caroly about it (she made this block) and we laugh about it to this day—only in New York!"

— JAN ROSENTHAL STEFURA

BABY QUILT FOR ROLLIE KREWSON'S DAUGHTER ARIANNA

Rollie's quilt has blocks featuring her interest in Maurice Sendak's art, her collection of baby bottles, plus a picture of a Victorian house (she and her husband both collect Victorian memorabilia). The Bunny in Bed block, made by Elena Pellicciaro, has a tiny removable stuffed bunny. Arianna was born before the quilt was finished, so her name and birthdate were embroidered in the heart block by Leigh Daley.

Dauntless Dragon

"Dauntless Dragon was the Muppet who almost didn't happen. He was originally a character for the TV special 'The Christmas Toy,' but as the script was rewritten Dauntless's role was cut back, and Rollie turned her talents to creating the remaining characters. But Rollie didn't forget about Dauntless. Of all the characters Rollie created, I chose this one because it shows her dauntless determination. She made this character during odd moments: waiting for paint to dry, during meetings. Despite his few moments on camera, the dragon added much to the look of the show. To me, the Dauntless Dragon block represents all the careful details and whimsy Rollie's dedication has added to the Muppets over the years."
—JOANNE GREEN

BABY QUILT FOR JODY SCHOFFNER'S SON OSCAR

Jody Schoffner worked as a costumer for *Sesame Street Live* for several seasons. This quilt was made by her coworkers to commemorate the birth of her son. The border on the quilt features the Ohio Star because that is where Jody lived at the time. The center block by Stephen Rotondaro served as the color inspiration for the quilt. The sashing fabric was taken, appropriately, from a costume for *Sesame Street Live*.

Sunshine

QUILTING WITH THE **MUPPETS**

BABY QUILT FOR LARRY JAMESON'S DAUGHTER MARY KIMBERLY

L arry works as a supervisor of the electro-mechanical department, and is responsible for many magical things including those times Kermit plays the banjo. Caroly Wilcox's block is a greeting from Larry's two sons, Alan and John, to their new baby sister. Fred Buchholz and his wife Helen Ripple collect labels and shared many to make make their quilt block. Ed Christie made one of his signature bug blocks—there are tiny blue and orange ants crawling all over the square.

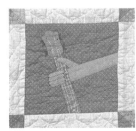

Kermit Playing the Banjo

"Larry Jameson is a gifted special-effects artist, who designs elaborate mechanisms that add much to the Muppet illusion. But not everyone remembers that he began in the company as a skilled woodworker who created wonderful props and musical instruments for the Muppets. Everything a Muppet handles must be specially made in a smaller scale. Larry's renditions of a classic Les Paul guitar and a Fender bass for the Electric Mayhem Band delight our audiences. One of the best Muppet moments is in The Muppet Movie, *when Kermit sits alone in his home swamp, playing his banjo. I wanted this moment, and this aspect of Larry's artistry, recorded in the quilt."*

—JOANNE GREEN

BABY QUILT FOR JOANNE GREEN'S SON DANTE

Joanne Green hung her quilt in her baby's room, on the wall next to the rocker, and felt surrounded by her friends. There are a number of distinctive blocks in the quilt. Paul Hartis created Snore Pie with Yawn Sauce to represent one of Joanne's sayings from the HBO series "Fraggle Rock." The Pew It's Mew square (by Rollie Krewson) shows a small catnip mouse puppet named Mew that Joanne created for the TV special, "The Christmas Toy."

Minivan with Shark and Flamingo

Danger: High Voltage

"During the taping of the special 'The Muppets Go to Disney World,' one of our production trailers caught fire. The fire trucks arrived, sirens wailing, and everyone was assured there had been no danger. We sighed with relief that no one had been hurt. As the fire trucks pulled away, we noticed with horror the melted 'Danger: High Voltage' sign on a nearby transformer. The block is a faithful representation of the melted sign, using cheerful but gray flowered fabrics."

— POLLY SMITH

"A few of us went to Disney World to shoot 'The Muppets Go to Disney World,' and they provided a van for our transportation. The security guard who let us in every day to the backstage area was too serious and strident. So we started adding more to the van: an inflatable shark and flamingo, chainette fringe, pompoms, and furry dice, so eventually the van resembled a day at the beach. We laughed— the guard didn't."

— MARK ZESZOTEK

Dutch Mushrooms

"Somehow chaos reigned supreme when Jitka [Exler] and I dutifully brought a few puppets to tape an ad for Dutch mushrooms. The Dutch producer demanded, in a thick accent, 'Where are the spectators? For the bleachers?' Apparently, hordes of Muppets were to cram stadium stands, cheering for the Dutch mushrooms. We scrambled to round up as many Muppet characters as we could find—virtually anything we could find in the workshop. 'And where are the vomen?' the producer demanded. As the main purchasers of Dutch mushrooms, women were not to be left out. Inspired, Jitka tied a head scarf around an especially gruesome monster puppet. In no time, we had lots of 'vomen.' Jitka made this block for me—it is machine embroidered, even the darling mushroom faces."

— JOANNE GREEN

BABY QUILT FOR JOHN BARRETT'S DAUGHTER BRIGITTE

John is the long-standing freelance photographer for The Jim Henson Company. He has shot most of the licensing, publishing, and publicity photographs for the past twenty years, as well as photos for this book. The quilt for John's daughter includes blocks that highlight the baby theme, as well as those that relate to his career and personal history. The square with the art arrows on it was done by Lauren Attinello, the art director on a number of John's photo shoots. Lyndon Mosse, an art director for the company, created the black square with two eyeballs and the words "It's Dark in Here"—what Lyndon would say to John to indicate that the camera lens was closed.

Baby Kermit with Camera

Shutterbug

"I'll admit I agonized over this quilt square because I've worked with John for more than 18 years, and I wanted to do something unique. I was stymied until I found the perfect pattern for a photographer. The title? Shutterbug! After I finished my square, I had a disconcerting moment when I discovered that Ed Christie had also done a Shutterbug for John's quilt. Take a look and see the two very different takes on the same title."

—DANIELLE OBINGER

"John is the ultimate Muppet photographer. Together we photographed Kermit hundreds of times, and I thought it would be appropriate for Kermit to return the favor. Because the quilt was for John's daughter, I used Kermit as a Muppet Baby. The lens in the camera is a clear piece of plastic that is removable for cleaning. Above Baby Kermit is the word HA!, because The Jim Henson Company was known as Henson Associates—HA—when John and I did most of our work together."

—JIM MAHON

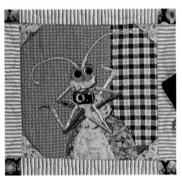

Shutterbug

It's Dark in Here

Baby Grouch

BABY QUILT FOR LISA HOWARD TOBIN'S SON CONNER

Lisa's quilt was made by a varied group of people. In addition to the people at the Muppet Workshop, fabric was sent to former coworkers, her two grandmothers who "signed" their blocks, and even friends from graduate school. Caroly Wilcox made the Miss Piggy block because she best remembers Lisa as the girl who built and costumed a human-sized Miss Piggy for "Muppet Show on Tour." Maria McNamara made a block of a girl tending a garden, since Lisa lived with Maria and her husband for a summer and often took care of their garden. Elena Pellicciaro created one of her signature "Bunny in Bed" blocks, because it had proven so popular in the quilt for Rollie Krewson's daughter Arianna.

Häagen Dazs

"I first met Lisa at New York University. One day during lunch, Lisa sat with a pint of Häagen Dazs and a spoon. When I asked her if she was going to eat the whole carton, she replied 'I didn't get this way by breathing.'"

— STEPHEN ROTONDARO

BABY QUILT FOR MARIA MCNAMARA'S DAUGHTER LUCY

Maria was a puppet builder in the Muppet Workshop for years. She collects wind-up toys, which is reflected in Joanne Green's block "Wind-up Dragon." Maria and her husband love to fly kites, which is represented by the Kites block. The Parakeet block harkens back to the day Maria got a very short haircut—she was told that she looked like a parakeet, and the name stuck. Maria's most memorable Muppets are the rats she made for the film *The Muppets Take Manhattan*.

Rat with Spool of Thread

"The block itself is the traditional Spool of Thread, but I used striped fabric to represent the thread and appliquéd a rat holding a threaded needle. Maria had just completed making a LOT of rats!"
— CAROLY WILCOX

BABY QUILT FOR JITKA EXLER'S SON NICHOLAS

Jitka Exler was a Czech puppet builder who worked first on the Czech "Sesame Street" show, and later in the New York Workshop. The American flag block is in honor of her U.S. citizenship. For his block, Stephen Rotondaro re-created a birthday card Jitka had made for Connie Peterson—the card featured the Czech animated characters Křemílek and Vochomůrka. The quilt is purple and black because those are Jitka's favorite colors. The layout of the quilt was unconventional, because so is Jitka.

Zondra

Zebra

"I chose Zondra for Jitka because, to me, Jitka and Zondra are one and the same. Same personality, same look. If ever there was a puppet designer who looked like her puppet, this is it.

Jitka loves asymmetry and I tried to get that in the background of the square. I used fleece for Zondra's skin and fur for her hair because I really wanted to get the essence of the real puppet."
—ROLLIE KREWSON

Krěmílek and Vochomůrka

American Flag for Jitka's Citizenship

Grasshopper

BABY QUILT FOR LARRY GALANTER'S DAUGHTER LAURA

Larry has been the Workshop accountant for the last ten years. He likes silly characters like clowns, so Mark Zeszotek made a square of "Mr. Blobby," an English television character for him. Larry also kept a fish tank in his office, so Jason Weber made a square in which a dead fish floats upside down in a tank. He used reverse appliqué for the water pattern and appliquéd fish from a fish print fabric.

Winston with Winning Ticket

"In some of the squares, I embroider-embellish portraits of the recipient's pet. Sometimes I work with a photo-graphic image I've printed from my computer, and sometimes I do an original drawing. The one in Larry Galanter's quilt is from an original drawing in which his dog destroys a winning lottery ticket, which is probably what would happen if Larry ever won "
— POLLY SMITH

Cookie Monster

"Cookie Monster has always been my favorite "Sesame Street" character. I love his wacky facial expression, with his wobbly, unfocused eyeballs and tooth-less, gaping maw. I also identify with his sweet tooth!"
— DAVID ROBERTS

BABY QUILT FOR ELLEN WALLOP'S SON WILL

Ellen Wallop was the photo assistant to John E. Barrett (The Jim Henson Company's long-time photographer). When Ellen and her husband, Michael, were expecting a baby they were surprised with this beautiful quilt, one of the smallest, yet most intricate, of all the friendship quilts made. Barbara Davis did much of the work on the quilt—she created all four "W" triangles, the "E" for Ellen, the "M" for Michael, as well as the scalloped border. Lyndon Mosse contributed a whimsical rendition of a Polaroid picture—one minute the film looks blank, then you lift the flap and a giggling baby appears.

Baby Polaroid

"Ellen worked with me for about five years. I watched her load film, adjust exposure, press buttons, and mostly 'rip' Polaroids. Professional Polaroid film still requires a developing time and the removal, or 'ripping' of a top sheet, or negative. What's interesting about this process is that you don't know what you're going to get until the top sheet is ripped—I thought this was a lot like being pregnant. My block represents this Polaroid. It's created in the exact proportions of the film, and only when you rip the little Velcro tab on the front is the adorable little baby revealed."
— LYNDON MOSSE

BABY QUILT FOR RICK VELLEU'S SON JESSE

Rick Velleu began his career at the Muppets as an assistant in the photo studio. One day during a photo shoot, coworkers decided to "help" Rick and Joy, his wife, name their as-yet-unborn child. They tacked a piece of paper on the studio door and produced a very long, and very ridiculous, list of names: Hullabaloo Velleu, Drew Velleu, Lulu Velleu, Skip-to-My-Lou Velleu . . . that list of silly names, like the quilt, was done with much love and affection for Rick and Joy.

Baby's First Scripts

"Rick began his career at the Muppets as my assistant, and soon proved himself a great talent and an even better friend. I was selfishly upset when he announced that he was returning to school to get a Master's degree in filmmaking. Suddenly his life was consumed by scripts. He was reading scripts, writing scripts, directing scripts. And so [the block I made for him] is 'Baby's First Scripts'—it's actually 'Baby's First Steps,' but I crossed out 'Steps' and overlaid the word 'Scripts' on top. It's a stack of pillowcases folded in half and stitched in the same way you would saddle stitch a pamphlet. I was lucky to find shirting fabric that looked exactly like lined paper, especially when top-stitched with a red margin. Hopefully Rick's son will one day fill the pages [of this book] with brilliant storytelling and take it to Hollywood."
— LYNDON MOSSE

QUILTING WITH THE **MUPPETS**

BABY QUILT FOR MARILEE CANAGA'S SON QUINT

Marilee Canaga's quilt was made while she was working on the TV show "Dinosaurs" so the inner border is dinosaurs in sunglasses. At the time, Marilee was also working nights maintaining a large hydraulic King Kong, so Marian Keating put the giant ape in her square. Joelle McGonagle made the beautiful beaded spider square, just because she knows Marilee's taste. The color scheme is very bright, as everyone in the Workshop knew that nothing was ever too loud or too bright for Marilee. She recalls the years surrounding her marriage, and the birth of her two sons, as being the happiest of her life. All the warm and playful memories surrounding that time are wrapped up in this beautiful quilt.

Sperm and Egg

"The show 'Dinosaurs' was truly magical. Most everyone was either falling in love, getting married, or making babies. I did all three. James Hayes recorded the moment in his square. It shows an egg and sperm, complete with a yellow feather for the sperm's tail."
— MARILEE CANAGA

BABY QUILT FOR MARIAN KEATING'S SON LIAM

Marian Keating worked in the New York Muppet Workshop for many years before joining the Los Angeles Creature Shop. She chose the colors for her quilt, and said she wanted it to look "like a garden of irises." Several people made iris squares using a variety of construction methods: appliqué, embroidery, and piecing.

Roger's Garage

"Roger, Marian's husband, has a garage piled high with leftover props from films, television shows, and commercials, so there is no room for anything else except their cat, Pie."
— JULIE ZOBEL

BABY QUILT FOR JULIE ZOBEL'S SON WOLFGANG

There are a number of themes prominent in Julie Zobel's quilt. Shooting stars are appliquéd, embroidered, and in prints. Flowers appear in both prints and appliqués. Elephants appear twice, as a reference to Julie's elephant ride in Nepal. Finally, there is a hidden message in the intersecting diamonds which reads: This quilt was made for Julie by her loving friends at the Muppets, Summer 1992.

Banana Slug

"Julie and I spent a very long, damp week in Oregon doing a photo shoot out-of-doors. The scenery was magnificent, but there were slugs—big slugs—everywhere. Bruce McNally, our art director, drew slug caricatures of each of us. The banana slug in my block wears a rainhat just like the khaki brimmed hat Julie wore that week."
—DANIELLE OBINGER

Glossary of Terms

Adhesives: Two common types are fusible and paper-backed adhesives. The fusible adhesive is used to adhere one fabric to another. Paper-backed adhesives adhere fabrics together, but have one adhesive side covered with paper for ease of use when tracing designs onto fabric.

Background Fabric: The background block fabric serves as a foundation to hold the appliqué pieces.

Lightbox: When you use a lightbox to transfer a pattern, the pattern goes on the bottom (illustration facing up) and the fabric background block goes on top. You may trace directly on the appliqué fabric using a fine pen or chalk as a marker.

Trapunto Method: Machine trapunto is used to achieve a "stuffed" (trapunto) look without having to cut holes in the back of your quilt (then stuff them), to give dimension to the top of the quilt. This technique was developed for machine quilters, but can also be used by hand quilters.

Soutache: A narrow, rounded braid woven from an odd number of threads used for trimming.

Stabilizers: Iron-on interfacing (including tear-away stabilizers), bonding, or light spray starch are used to make a base fabric a bit stiffer and easier to handle. They are also used to stiffen the cut edges of small appliqué pieces to reduce fraying and edge disintegration caused by the needle's action. Common tear-away adhesives are used to stiffen the background fabric for stitching, then are pulled away from the fabric to reduce bulk once stitching is completed.

Index of Artists

For more information write
for a free catalog:
C&T Publishing, Inc.
P.O. Box 1456
Lafayette, CA 94549
(800) 284-1114
http://www.ctpub.com
e-mail: ctinfo@ctpub.com

For quilting supplies:
Cotton Patch Mail Order
3405 Hall Lane, Dept. CTB
Lafayette, CA 94549
e-mail: quiltusa@yahoo.com
http://www.quiltusa.com
(800) 835-4418